The Familiar Wild
On Dogs & Poetry

Sundress Publications • Knoxville, TN

Copyright © 2020
ISBN: 978-1-951979-02-7
Library of Congress: 2020930999
Published by Sundress Publications
www.sundresspublications.com

Editors: Ruth Awad and Rachel Mennies

Editorial Assistants: Anna Black and Erin Elizabeth Smith

Editorial Interns: Nicole Drake, Erica Hoffmeister, Quinn Carver Johnson, Kanika Lawton, Kimberly Ann Priest, Sabrina Sarro, and Jacquelyn Scott

Colophon: This book is set in Bell MT.

Cover Design: Lori Tennant

Cover Image: Shineprint

Book Design: Erin Elizabeth Smith

The Familiar Wild
On Dogs & Poetry
Edited by Ruth Awad and Rachel Mennies

Contents

Introduction — 13

C. SINCLAIRE BROWN
Ars Poetica — 15
Ode to the Bullet-Gouged Eye — 17

CANDACE WILLIAMS
Crown Heights — 19

HANIF ABDURRAQIB
Watching A Fight At The New Haven Dog Park, First Two Dogs, And Then Their Owners — 21
What a Miracle That Our Parents Had Us When They Could Have Gotten A Puppy Instead — 23

CARLY JOY MILLER
I've Given Myself to the Dogs — 24

MAGGIE SMITH
Walking the Dog — 25
The Village Dogs — 27

CHLOE HONUM
The Ward Above — 28
Phoebe — 29

M. SOLEDAD CABALLERO
Of Names and Numbers — 30

CHEN CHEN
a small book of questions: chapter x ... 31
ode to my beloveds & brevities ... 33

ROBIN BECKER
Rescue Riddle ... 36
Where the Unfairness of the World Resides ... 37
Xenia ... 38

TARA BETTS
If It Wasn't For a Dog, We'd Have No Woof Tickets ... 39

ROSALIE MOFFETT
New Evidence of Water ... 40
Something Quiet ... 42
How is She? I Don't Say I Am Afraid ... 44

BRUCE SNIDER
Devotions ... 45

RAENA SHIRALI
PASTORAL WITH KEYS CLENCHED, AS A WEAPON, IN MY FIST ... 50

NOAH BALDINO
On Trust ... 51
Pep Talk ... 53

ALI SHAPIRO
Dogs in Love ... 55

IRÈNE P MATHIEU
there is no word for (my mother's fear of everything that might touch me) ... 56

EMILY ROSE COLE
Lovebites — 58

JASON MYERS
Spies — 59

LIZ BOWEN
Poor Stress Tolerance 1 — 61
Poor Stress Tolerance 2 — 62

EMILIA PHILLIPS
My Dog Refused to Go Near the Dead Rabbit in the Backyard — 64

LINDA DOVE
The Dog Poem — 66

KUNJANA PARASHAR
Ritual — 67

STEVEN CORDOVA
Sissy Boy — 68

LIZA FLUM
Domestication — 69

GRADY CHAMBERS
Black Pomeranian — 71

LISA FAY COUTLEY
Leash Training — 72
What Have You — 73
Forgiveness — 76

RUTH BAUMANN
I'm Thirty Now, Poem 78
Reassurances 80

NINA SUDHAKAR
Commands in Progress 81
At Night 82

CRISTINA ANNINO as translated by ADRIA BERNARDI
Il cane del buon consiglio / The Advice-Giving Dog 84

KELLI RUSSELL AGODON
Hunger 86

MATTHEW GAVIN FRANK
After Grano Maturo 87

SAGE RAVENWOOD
Can't Branch 89

CARRIE SHIPERS
The History of Dogs 91

JENNIFER PERRINE
In This Dog-Eat-Dog World 92

LEILA ORTIZ
Blessed 94

BECCA BARNISKIS
Saint Mutt 95

JEANNE WAGNER
Dogs That Look Like Wolves 96

JEFF OAKS
The Black Dog in the Middle of the Night   98

SALLY ROSEN KINDRED
Earth Science   101

AMY WATKINS
Clarity   103

JULIA STORY
The Last in a Series of Dog Elegies   104
Barking   105

ASHLEY INGUANTA
Two Notes From a Far Off Watchdog   106

SARAH LUX
Fleet Week   108

NOMI STONE
Waiting for Happiness   110

Author Essays   111

Contributors   123

Reprint Credits   133

Thank You   135

Editors   137

To our dogs, alive and gone, who have made our worlds kinder and possible.

Introduction

Rachel: Otto is sleeping beside me: forty-odd pounds of mixed greyhound and other-, warming my feet as winter arrives in Chicago. His ongoing, grounding presence has kept me on the planet for yet another calendar year. He sighs loudly, a burden-free sigh, the sort of sigh I've always wanted to sigh.

I don't know how else to say it without the edges softening into pablum—for nearly seven years now, the dog has kept me alive. In trade, I have lovingly kept the dog (my first) alive. My brain, chugging constantly into broken, compromised futures as a symptom of my obsessive-compulsive disorder, takes instruction from Otto's brain, which surveys the present only for comfort and for his companion. My mind finds peace next to his mind; it finds a purpose there. As a poet, the rituals of his care—the walking, the feeding, the resting—stabilize my writing practice. These daily tasks don't inspire me to write, per se (not often, at least), but they keep the door to my life open so that I might walk through this door—and the one to the next day, and the next—without fear.

*

Ruth: My first dog Pete came into my life when I was only 19 and recovering from sexual assault and addiction. I was trying to put myself back together when this small, moon-eyed Pomeranian made me try harder—if not for myself, then to keep her alive. I had to stop drinking myself numb because I couldn't be blackout drunk and mindful of her safety. I couldn't sleep through the day because she needed to be let out and fed. She was so small that she would have hypoglycemic seizures if she didn't eat on time every day, and dear reader, I did find that out once the hard way. But it wasn't the routine of her care alone that was essential to my survival. I had a companion to sit with me through each moment, the unbearable and the blissful. With her, I could face the ongoing minutes, and eventually, years.

Pete and I lived 11 years together. I have four dogs now, some who had the fortune to overlap with Pete's life, others who know her only through the caregiving she helped forge. I think all the time about how her companionship made me consider my life outside of myself. That it has value to others and maybe for that reason, I should also value it.

*

When we first had the idea to undertake this anthology, on a warm summer evening in Pittsburgh, we knew other poets who loved their dogs as we did, which is to say, rapturously and unendingly. What we didn't know enough about—and wanted desperately to know more—was how other poets depicted those familiar, wild creatures in their poems. A project begun by Ruth's *Pet Poetics* interview series, which explores the animal-artist connection and animals' influence on artists' creative practices, took root in that moment and grew over a couple of years of scheming, reading, and talking into life the anthology you're holding in your hands right now.

While anthologies of dog poems have existed for a long, long time, we wanted to create room for writers usually overlooked on this subject. We know through our own experiences and social circles that dog companionship occupies an essential space in the lives of marginalized folx. What would we learn if we invited that intersectional conversation? Maybe we could move beyond the stories we're used to hearing and into a terrain as familiar and unknowable as our own need for companionship.

For many of the poets in this collection, there exists no poetry without dogs. As contributor C. Sinclaire Brown writes of her rescue dog Tillie: "When I adopted [Tillie], I had to put myself aside, listen to her, learn her language, her fears, how to talk to her in a way that she could understand. The whole process has taught me how to re-evaluate my own work, the work of writing into what is truly mysterious and terrifying and baffling, and letting myself simply be mystified, terrified, baffled." We can imagine no other mode, whether of poetry or life, more necessary than attending to this mutual bafflement alongside our animal companions.

Thank you for venturing here with us. We hope you leave different than you arrived.

C. SINCLAIRE BROWN

Ars Poetica

it's summer, summer everywhere.
hot bodies cooling and thrashing in big water.
young people gay and alive and shining
and more or less in love
depending on their star signs.
light fracturing across the universe like a weed
breaking through concrete.
lovers throwing their bodies into the seams
of one another, stitching with gold thread.
writers are putting their dogs in their poems
knowing they will outlive their dogs.
that if they put their dogs in their poems
the dogs will still die. still: to write a poem
is a forward motion. if you are alive
another day and another day, that, too,
is a forward motion. retrograde
is an optical illusion. mercury is always
spinning forward on its track. everyone dies,
the lovers say to each other. you know
that it happens. it breaks your heart
every time. but they keep on doing it,
fucking and shining and partitioning the light.
unstitching themselves, the gold thread
catching fire. someone says,
the only thing faster than light is the flash
-bang of each synapse snapping in your head
telling you the world is right
here, happening, right now. that you've already

entered the future where you are still alive
whether you want to be or not.
no matter how long it takes to find love or to die
it will feel like forever. even the stars
will be dying forever, each gaseous heart
pulling its whole body, every body around it,
impossibly close. somewhere on earth
a woman stands with her face
to the curtains, a strand of light
dribbling into her mouth. she swallows, tasting
air. her lover is gone and it's still summer
everywhere. a dog moves stiffly into the room.
she pours water into a glass and thinks
of dog poems. then she opens the curtains.
light breaks in through the kitchen window.
love falls all over the floor.

C. SINCLAIRE BROWN

Ode to the Bullet-Gouged Eye

& the bird it belonged to & the frantic jaw of the dog that finds it
—winged & wounded & warbling thing—& wraps it
in tongue & teeth & spit—its whole & holy hot dark dog-mouth—& carries it back as offering
through the weedy slick & browning scrub, through the whole wet marshland,
pulled happily by the scruff by love & duty, down the clear-tunneled path
of his hunter's whistle, call of homegoing, call of praise—*good boy, good boy, look
  what you've brought me, look what you've done—*
      another fresh-dead thing, bright-bloodied & perfect:

what a picture of pride & power & quick-drawn fear & allegiance & ache & joy—

---

            sometimes i feel myself the bird,
    struck & gasping, hurtling toward earth, warbling & warbling:

      o wound, o wind, o sopping country: bring me a god
worth the eye i have lost, all this injustice, the long fall & the dark
    humid journey in this tooth-lined boat, worth the shore
      i will not meet, the glittery song i was singing—

      give my bird-bones a softer landing next time; give me
        gold-lined feathers & broader wings;
a clear throat like that tall figure that whistles & whistles; a long wind
     that won't end & a love like the one i feel in this heat,
       in the breath of this heaving beast—

o god of fowl & fouling: make me bright
& starry, next time, too swift & too far to shoot down again;

may i never blink out of the wild sky again.

CANDACE WILLIAMS

Crown Heights

She pulls the curtain back and light engulfs
her pre-war home. The sun illuminates
the parquetry and lines of lacquered oak
around the walls. The kettle boils; she grinds
the coffee beans and weighs the grounds. She drinks
her coffee while she reads the *Times*. She puts
her pit bull into coat and boots. They do
their morning routine—heading west on Crown
to Rogers; turning right and buying sweets
near President; going east to Nostrand
and walking back to Crown. She walks the heart
of Crown Heights. She walks the ghost perimeter
of Crow Hill Castle—named after murders
of crows that flocked to trees atop the hill;
or darkies lined up on the hill like crows;
or the louring inmates dressed in crow black.
She's never heard of this Crow Hill because
the county tore it down and built Crown Heights.
The county built and ran the Castle too.
The walls were pitched thirty feet high and made
of stone. Eight turrets enclosed five acres.
Women were jailed with infants in their cells.
The men were forced to dig the city roads.
The women stitched; they sewed 15,000
leather shoes per day. The Sabbath sermon
would ring from chapel under sobs and screams
of men and women whipped with frayed cowhide.
The inmates starved or had to eat the bad
food—rancid butter, rotted fish and meat.

That was then. Now, a CrossFit gym is named Crow Hill and there's a coffee shop that's called *Colina Cuervo,* where she likes the croissants.

HANIF ABDURRAQIB

Watching A Fight At The New Haven Dog Park, First Two Dogs,
And Then Their Owners

The mailman still hands me bills like I should be lucky to have my name on anything in this town & I been here 14 months & all I get is paper telling me who I owe & when I owe them & what might be taken from me if I don't hand over the faces of dead men & I love the electric architecture of noise on the corner of Chapel & State where the old dudes who drown their afternoons in warm liquid build porches from neon glass & yell I see you boy at the Yale kids who walk by dressed in salmon colored windbreakers regardless of whether or not the wind is present or asking to be broken & I, too, dress for the hell I want & not the hell that is most likely coming & at the fence outside the dog park my own dog pulls towards home & all of my dogs pull towards home & I am a leash sometimes & I send flowers to funerals from 3 states away now & I'm saying that which forces us to bare our teeth is all a matter of perspective & inside the dog park a game of fetch has gone awry & the dog that looks like a wheat field is circling the dog that looks like a melted ice cream cone & the wheat field is all teeth & the melted cone is a trembling mess & when the stakes are most violent I suppose we all become what we resemble most & what I mean is that the men on the corner are only drunks until the cops come & then they are scholars & I am from the kind of place where no one makes a fist if they aren't going to throw the thing & when the wheat field lunges, the melted cone knows what's what & sidesteps the glistening teeth with impeccable precision & I can't believe that all of this is over a stick but I imagine that to a dog, a stick is an entire country & surely I've thrown hands in the name of less & the dogs have owners & the owners are chest to chest & yelling at each other about which dog started the fight that is a fight in name only, the wheat field dog lunging & missing & lunging & missing & I feel guilty when I start to hope that the dog owners throw a punch at each other just so I can remember what it looks like when a fist determines its own destiny & I haven't seen a real fight since Chris from Linden mopped up some kid from the suburbs back in '02 outside of the Dairy Queen after the kid had one too many jokes about Chris' pops catching 25 years on the back of some real shit & Chris knocked that boy out so fast he ain't even get touched & we carried Chris home with his clean face & clean hands & so I really don't have the time for all of the theater at this dog park & I am getting too old & I want only a good dog most days & I'm saying I want a dog that will never ask me to finish something it started & I'm saying I want a dog that will never make me clean its blood out of the streets.

HANIF ABDURRAQIB

What A Miracle That Our Parents Had Us When They Could Have Gotten
A Puppy Instead

i guess it is good to know you are needed by something that won't outgrow you. or that won't learn a name to call you outside of. i am back to wearing sweaters in summer. it's a question of intimacy. that which will do the work of love for those who have grown weary of loving me. every four years in america it becomes fashionable to make promises you can't keep and so here i am again. i tell you that i will try to make it to your brunch/reading/karaoke night and then i draw a blanket over my chest and look to see who will deliver me something warm. i hold a face in my palms and turn it towards a field of sunflowers, their bright ridges arched into the night's humid mouth. i say *i will always be here, as i am now* and the true lie is that time doesn't already have its talons in all of our backs, pulling a younger version of ourselves thrashing to the gates after each passing hour. i am lying, too, about my dog and what the years have done to her. i am lying about this though I see the way she eyes the flight of steps at the opening of our home. she makes it up them, yes, but then gasps over a water bowl. nothing is like it was in the old days, they say. everything outside is dying easier. melting. the answer to thirst as our undoing. i take up whatever space i must and apologize later. in the mirror, i am already vanishing. it's the need to be loved that we'll all miss most. my dog doesn't always run when i call her name. i don't always reply to my father's texts.

CARLY JOY MILLER

I've Given Myself to the Dogs

who gift their sleep to the sunspot
on the couch. The couch bears such
functional weight: Supports the human
and creature, doesn't know it's a landscape
because the humans name it so: *Blanket
mountain, unfurled blanket river, sunshine
ledge.* Depending on weight, the backs
of the couch fall off. It's treacherous,
the dogs passing over, jumping off the ledge.
We know where they land. But where
do their minds go? Sniffing is a kind
of knowledge-making. I don't rush
their learning our home's corners,
the same poles over and over. Why deny
them a multi-scented world? I've leashed
myself to their wonder. I would kill
to track every second of joy.

MAGGIE SMITH

Walking the Dog

If I saw myself walking down Roosevelt Avenue
this morning, what would I think of that woman,

40ish, hauling her dog on a leash—*no, leave it,
leave it, good girl*—her two kids dawdling behind,

found sticks in hand, whining about the heat,
the pavement already silvery? I'd think her left palm—

my left palm—is raw where the leash cuts in,
the terrier pulling, insistent, nose to the ground.

What is she on to? That a scent sliced its way
through this too-thick air is reason enough to

follow it. What is she on to now? I mean the woman.
I mean me. What does she follow by instinct alone?

What does she refuse to be tugged away from,
the woman I hardly know on the street

or in the mirror, hair parted on the wrong side,
pink mole on the opposite cheek? I know the mirror

has something to do with recognition, but today
I think it has everything to do with the critic in me

who cringes to say *recognition*. If I saw myself
walking the dog, seeing is all I could offer. Look,

that's me, coaxing my wilted kids down the block,
the pavement already shimmering like a burn.

MAGGIE SMITH

The Village Dogs

I have heard of places where
dogs leave their homes one by one
in the morning and meet up in the streets.
They lie together in the park, freckled

bellies warming in the sun, then leave
for the butcher's, for alley-scraps
of ham, chorizo, a bit of blood
sausage they needn't even beg for.

The butcher carves with village dogs
in mind. They come daily for the salt
of cured meats. I wonder if they lap
the savory sea air, too, the way

the silver-bearded black Lab
of my childhood licked the halo
of cigarette smoke from around
my mother, as if to help us see her.

I have heard of places where
dogs roam free—no dogcatchers,
no meddling neighbors. I hesitate
to call their ritual togetherness *family*,

but what is family? At sundown
the dogs come home one by one.
Inside, they click across the tiles.
No one even needs to call them.

CHLOE HONUM

The Ward Above

I don't need to look up to know that inside some of the fluorescent lights there are dead flies on their backs, their wings at crisp diagonals. The psychiatrist has a face like an old dictionary. I imagine myself in the ward above, for the more severe cases. I'm afraid I'll float up and ask to be admitted. In the common room, the Vietnam vet says, *No, you don't want to go up there.* Everything he says, he says again with his eyes. At home, my dog sleeps beside me. She groans as I slide my hand beneath her head. I speak to her. I carry her warm, happy skull through the night.

CHLOE HONUM

Phoebe

At the clinic, a nurse taps my veins and they find their tiny voices. Blood sweeps into the vial and a chunk of snow slides from my boot. The shine on the linoleum floor is brutal, but no one is saying so. Outside, it is both noon and evening, as if winter were trying to be giving. In the parking lot: a hooded woman. You want to know what I believe? I believe my dog would come between my death and me, that she would come huffing and shaking all over, as her dreams allow.

M. SOLEDAD CABALLERO

Of Names and Numbers

Frieda was Molly when we got her.
Who knows what she was before that.
Left behind when a man claimed the other two
but not her, gangly, thin, dark like pond water,
black holes, and soot. We picked her out
from the rows of cages lining the hallway.
She had no sounds, only breath. She said nothing.
She was silence and eyes. We brought her home,
half starved, swampy eyed, her coat matted,
dull from illicit days outside. She endured
the car ride pressed small into the corner
of the Subaru, resigned. We called her Frieda.
thinking of the Frida of skeleton dreams, industrial
bleeding and paint. But Frieda had no visible scars,
no bright, oil-based sadness. She had only a number,
faded blue inside her right ear, a tattoo before
she was Molly or Frieda, a tattoo before she was.
In thirteen years, we never learned the numbers.
They did not matter. On her last day, we called
her Frieda, like we did on her first. On her last day,
she knew her name.

CHEN CHEN

a small book of questions: chapter x
    after Bhanu Kapil

& what would you say if you could?

She asks about the dog before she asks about the boyfriend.

She doesn't ask about him. She does this for a year.

Will do this for years. Even after the boyfriend & I move back to the Northeast. Even when we're living ten minutes away & she comes to our apartment with an ugly vase I suspect she is regifting. I accept it because she has also brought a large container full of green beans fried with garlic. She looks at the dog, seems to have an easier time looking at the dog, than looking at the boyfriend, the boyfriends, us. I want to say, *Mom, look. Ask*

about us. She asks about the dog.

        (*How's his hair? Everywhere?*)

Then I remember—about a year before we're ten minutes away, we come over from Rochester. We join my brother's college graduation lunch at Mu Lan in Waltham. & we're part of a party of six, eating as a party of twelve. The boyfriend goes to the restroom. She goes back to the dishes, which are somehow not finished, yet. She's not. She's picking up two magnificently crispy scallion pancakes—their full magnificence held between her chopsticks, her skillfully nonchalant grip—& then she's placing them on the boyfriend's plate. She looks at me. Says, *For him.*

Maybe she is asking about us by asking about the dog.

> (Or she asks about the dog because he is cuter than the boyfriend, cuter than the son, we might as well all be regifted vases compared to the dog.)

She says, *He likes the pancakes, he should have more.*

& what would she say if she could

say, be more? & what am I looking for, exactly? Do I look at her, the way she would like? Have I said *I love you* recently—the exact words, yes, but what about the exact foods? Couldn't we ask each other for more?

At the least, I want to remember better. Earlier this summer, she asks if he's coming over with me, for the 4th. She's making hotdogs & hamburgers, wants to know if she needs to make veggie burgers. For the boyfriend. *For him.* For some reason I think dinner, not lunch, so say, *Sure, we'll both come once he finishes with work.*

She's disappointed when he can't come.

She doesn't say disappointed. Says, *Take*

the veggie ones, & puts them in a large container, & that into a very large bag. Always these containers & bags, large & small & larger. She probably has something large enough, vast enough to carry all the hair the dog sheds, will ever shed.

> (I want to remember better. But I want more, more of the better to remember.)

She sighs in the midafternoon heat & I see the sweat on her face, then the lines.

Don't forget, she says, pointing to the bag with the veggie burgers. *For him.*

CHEN CHEN

ode to my beloveds & brevities

& beautiful jorts & beautifuler

pug breaths & the best of sandra

bullock & a slice of watermelon bursting

between the teeth of a boy in a bathtub

in an unmistakably ren hang photograph & you

are back home & you

are my favorite unabridged

absurdity & you

& i & why don't we start in this bed

the next big greater boston sandra

oh fan club & yes let's think

trees in late december

while we embrace & yes believe

them to be an abundance

of baldnesses & no

two the same & every one a blast & a half

& another half & the last poem i tried to write about

our no longer puppy but

always our baby just went like

!!!

& with a jiggly leap into the bed here he is

& what could be more

breathgiving than these pugly (meaning

beautifulest) wrinkles & nostrils &

couldn't we just gobble

up our little never bashful

buddy's ears

but wait i'm not supposed to say that

with my chinese breath

but (& eternally) fuck that

isn't this a fantabulous day & isn't his smile very

dog & aren't the three of us the busiest

goofballs & the strangest heartthrobs

& the gabbiest unstrangers &

some abracadabra mixed

with kablooey & unbamboozled

except by each other & fantabulously

pugly & oh

& so & gobbleable & &

& &

&

& & & & &

& why should we ever leave this bed

our breaths

ROBIN BECKER

Rescue Riddle

When she takes her morning tea, he settles
beside her—body of law and praise,
procuress, his winter and summer hearth.
Each day, for work, she turns her back
on his slim muzzle, narrow rib cage,
small paws braced. She might have left
him to starve with his brothers years ago
on that beach in Mexico, one leave-taking
instead of the thousands ahead of them.

ROBIN BECKER

Where the Unfairness of the World Resides

Into his bolstered bed, he withdraws,
a nautilus closing
up shop with a leathery hood. *Who*

rescued whom? the bumper sticker asks
five days after
the massacre in Orlando, where, six

states away, I drive him to the vet
who confirms he's going
blind and deaf. Oh, parchment-colored dog,

your fearful growl at my approach reveals
the original cruelties
we could never erase but held at bay

for years—like papyrus tightly scrolled. Derangement
of your senses and mistrust beset you,

leave me to leave you alone, delicate
paws shielding the face
where the unfairness of the world resides.

ROBIN BECKER

Xenia

Most days that summer your old dog came up,
in the searing heat, with a failing heart,
from your place, the half-mile uphill to mine—

up the steep rise, past the pastured goats, on
the buggy trail that swerves through blueberries.

As you pointed out, *The Odyssey*
is full of tears, everyone weeping
to find and lose and find each other again.

Spent, he struggled the last two hundred yards,
ears low, chest heaving. Hearing
the jangling of his tags I knew the gods

had chosen me to praise him for his journey,
offer food and water, a place to sleep.

TARA BETTS

If It Wasn't For a Dog, We'd Have No Woof Tickets

That chained up dog that keeps barking
even though it's toothless and too tired
to run. Yeah, one pretending it's brutal.
That dog ain't biting no damn body.

Yet it keeps slobbering and woofing
all the hollow threats and no chomp.
No strain on the tether, no snapping.
Just half a howl to shake an intruder.

So, when you grow up hearing about
woof tickets, a bill for a beating that
won't ever come, there ain't a single
tooth bared for all the booming bark
won't cash, so the ticket booth shuts
down early when a dog does more
than growl, ready to write the checks.

ROSALIE MOFFETT

New Evidence of Water

It was a mistake, perhaps,
to pick the most loyal breed of dog.
The day, after all, is always breaking

into two or more pieces: war,
postwar, etc. We occupy ourselves,

the dog and I, with the news
of our incredible luck: our tiny orbit
at the Goldilocks distance from the sun

where water is neither frozen
nor steam. Everything else

is an uninhabitable zone.
Which must be what I'm looking at every time
I look into the distance, or into the laptop

which is a kind of distance, its own
telescopic view

not only into space, but also
of a gutted tank, of a woman in a green dress
climbing out of a pile of cinder blocks.

The buildings on earth seem to be either
flattened or huge, depending. In other news, some horizon

has a nick in it, which means there may

have been water, once, on the moon. On TV
a boat parts the great Pacific trash vortex

only for a second. I think we must
want to leave

except gravity so loves us we can't
help but love the world
we made and all its shadows.

One follows me around
like a dog.

ROSALIE MOFFETT

Something Quiet

My mother's dog is buried under a railroad tie
    in the garden
because if there's not something heavy

    there, something quiet
will come and dig it up. My dog was cremated
    because I wanted to bury him

but where in my rented city yard
    could I? *I hope you know
I'm donating my body to science.* I'm about as far

    as I can go and be
in the same country as my mother,
    who is almost at the end

of the winding highway connecting the town
    to *nowhere*:
a hollowed canyon and its black cows, its river

    enameled with whatever
light the time of day is making. As soon as I held
    the dog's expensive ashes,

I knew it was an absurd question,
    where he'd want to be
scattered—couldn't walk myself

    through his dog-logic,
his trying to grasp what it mattered what I did
    with his body when he was

no longer in it. *Who knows what, then,*
    they'll learn about me,
what a specimen I'll be. The country is vast.

    I left home, drove away
towing a U-Haul. The world is full
    of beauty, is enormous.

It doesn't make a bit of difference
    where I put any
of the ones I've loved.

ROSALIE MOFFETT

How Is She? I Don't Say I Am Afraid

that I may soon hear of something final,
        some certain
end-date. *How* is she—I employ a polite

        veer-away: *She remains
in high spirits.* Or *Her lemon tree is blooming.*
        Or *Her dog excels in agility class.*

Which is true: her dog can, at long last, be coaxed
        into the narrow tunnel
with one cloth end collapsed,

        a thing designed for this sole purpose:
to appear to have no exit. No dog
        likes the way it looks.

One way to do it is to army-crawl in, yourself,
        a treat in your pocket.
Certain dogs will follow and certain dogs will meet you

        at the other end.
But my mother could not crawl, could not
        show the dog

it was possible to enter the dead-end,
        and find a way out.
I don't know what she did, but I watch now

        how she can say *In*, and point.
And the dog crawls in.

BRUCE SNIDER

Devotions

1.

Nothing passes, Lord, but what you allow.
Mornings the milky sap on my knuckles
burns. Last night the piglets fought then suckled
in the barn. Still no word. Our one cow
grazes but won't come in. The pamphlets say:
Patience is required. I say, let's try again
but John blames the state, the neighbors, the way
we wrote our bios, filling out the forms.
Across the road our neighbor starts his truck
while God, feather by feather, downs a wren—
swollen, its black eyes shiny, small dark tongue.
In the drainpipe, something slithers wet and stuck.
A racerunner? A ground skink shedding skin?
Lizards, John tells me, *can't bear live young.*

2.

John tells me: *lizards can't bear live young.*
Another of God's mysteries: hard rain
muddying the corn. The kind woman
at the agency said, *it takes longer for same-
sex couples.* Trash smoke rises like prayer,
the neighbor burning insulation from his shed.
He shows his son how to bind fence where
a crippled chicken pecks at scattered feed.

They talk, lean close. Rusted toys fill
the side yard: old trucks, a bicycle tire,
a punctured red bucket now a sieve.
In the back acre, ram mounts ewe, the whole
field coupling late spring. When John walks by,
I kiss him. Most days we keep to ourselves.

3.

I kiss him most days. We keep to ourselves
by the roadside. Two greasy boxes; a sign:
FREE. We take the runt, her warm body beside
us in the truck, milk-breathed and unwormed.
I imagine her shuddering out of the womb, wet
ground covered with slime. Strange to think
of her moving inside some animal's gut,
the source of each day's warm alien kick.
At home John makes her a bed from old
field shirts, a soap and vinegar bath for fleas
while in my lap she chews my hand and shivers.
I brush her fuzzy scruff, the too-large head.
She nips at my finger that holds a piece of cheese,
her wet tongue asking what a man can mother.

4.

Even I doubt how a man can mother
when I see the neighbor shout, chuck a stone
at his son. When I shoot him a look, he turns:
mind your own business. The hot sun withers
the peonies John planted on the side of the hill,
dirt gone hard with the sudden change of weather.

Sweating, I mow the lawn, pick up shell
casings in the yard, the crow's strict feathers.
All day, I want to break something, stick
a fork in the fan blades to feel the pinch.
Coming home late again from the shop,
John carries two rabbits slung from a hook.
He cleans, for hours, his rifle on the porch.
Above us: the moon rises. An easy shot.

5.

Above us the sun rises, bright and hot,
steaming the back pond where black flies stall.
In the pasture, our neighbor castrates his bulls
using a spreading tool with red rubber slats.
The restless cattle graze an unshorn meadow.
On TV: a baby in Toledo in a locked car.
The mother went to work and forgot, windows
up in summer's heat. The camera blurs
over the lot as a medic lifts the blanketed heap
from the back seat in the crew's full view.
Gawkers circle. The mother weeps. Watching,
I can peaches, letting the pale fruit darken.
Beyond the window, bulls still graze the field.
They feed. The bloodless sacks swing, blacken.

6.

Steer feed. The bloodless sacks hang, blackened.
On the radio: Haggard's *I'd rather be gone*.
John tends to ordinary things: replaces the drain
pipe in the kitchen sink, sharpens knives again.

I watch the neighbor teach his son to paint
the tool shed all afternoon. Soon, they wrestle,
throw a ball, the boy laughing into his father's chest.
In the paper I read the births and deaths,
hear a sudden hammering from behind,
John cursing the warped floorboards, pushing hard
the back door, which still won't budge an inch.
Again, today no miracles at hand,
just, in the field, wrens who stab at milkweed pods,
a nuthatch bargaining from its split branch.

7.

A nuthatch bargains from its split branch.
Our neighbor stops by, complains our fence
breaks his field. It must be moved eight inches.
The puppy—*Annie* we call her—pushes
her nose in everything, the front yard, the garden,
finds, across the road, the neighbor's trash—
drags stripped wire, egg shells that harden
like the bones she buries off his porch.
I want to say we are consoled by her,
but each day John jumps when he hears the phone.
We walk over and over down the worn
path to the empty mailbox: *Maybe soon.*
Some nights we make love. We sleep arm to arm.
We wake to our neighbor yelling at his son.

8.

Again, we wake, our neighbor yelling at his son,
poor kid standing by the porch. Tracking mud,

he backs from the shouting, his father's raised fist.
Later, I will see him sulking near our feed shed,
knotting an old piece of garden hose, kicking dust.
I'll smile, ask if he's o.k. But right now,
I listen to John's quiet breathing beside me.
Faith, they say, is Abraham asked to slaughter
his boy on a mountaintop. But sometimes
it's just the peeling shed in gray weather,
the leather harness softened, then gone rough.
All day today, the back pond will teem with carp.
The clover will brighten. For now, we lie together
into late morning. Some days, it is enough.

RAENA SHIRALI

PASTORAL WITH KEYS CLENCHED, AS A WEAPON, IN MY FIST

how the fat pink blossoms smell of sex & the season
when girls all cower has passed. onward

in the dimming light, i hold the dog close to my side
with a tether. i am followed by such a train of *oohs* &
before me the white boys on the fourth floor unfurl

their only emblem, their same-colors-as-acceptable-
pride—reconfiguration of stripes to flatten. what women

should wear & how : what a country should wear
& when. if i wrap myself in flags or if i wrap myself
in many warnings. if i point to the dog at my side

when making eye contact with any of the same
type who have held me against a brick wall. how the fat

squirrels don't duck when the dog lunges
toward them, & i think without thinking : *another species
asking to die.* fat pink blossom, sex emblem,

pepper-spraying my way through america—i am
my survival instinct or i am not

my survival instinct. daily i learn : reconfigure the self
as almost-not-killable, almost-not-
fuckable. keep walking & take stock of my

surroundings. only dead girls check their phones.
i am a fat pink sex symbol. i agree with you.

NOAH BALDINO

On Trust

When I reach for my rain jacket draped over the armchair,
Fanny flinches so hard that she falls to the floor. I can't explain

that I won't hit her. Not while her elbows still bleed
from that blanketless cage she spent her old life in—

her whole life, till last week. Until last week
she had never seen a couch before. I had to bring soft things to her,

carry cushions and duvets to the corner she'd staked
and refused to leave, not even to pee,

my jeans urine-dark at the knees every night; she faced the wall
while between shoulder blades I applied her flea medication. The shelter

said she's shy, but that's only half right—yes, she spooks
when aluminum peals off the molding because she eats so hard she rattles

the bowl. But that first night, after I'd pointed, pleading *couch, couch,*
and had lifted her, leg by hesitant leg, saying *feel that, it's the same*

as stairs, remember stairs, hoisting her bony butt up like one child helps another
clamber over a fence, nipping jaws at their heels, this dog I'd prayed would

choose me as the first she'd believe— me who needs, so selfishly,
someone's believing—rested, finally, her massive head in my lap. The weight of it

undeniable as rain to a roof. As mange to fur. I can't say
I won't hit her, since harmlessness isn't a height

you can reach, the last detached rung pencil-etched on the doorframe.
It's more like a muscle, worked—then rested. The rest is

what scares me the most. How many times have I fetched
the rope-toy of my anger just to thrash it as soon as

a friend comes too close? Beloved, you've seen me
spend whole weeks in tense stupor, each *I'm sorry, whoever,* bones beneath

the backyard. Why are you here now, bringing soup that you made me
even after I've listened far less than I've loved? For some of us, fear cedes

the body to stillness. For others, it's more a cruel heat you lose
track of, scalding any hand, burning the bottoms of pots. Fanny yawns,

sleep-settled. Her tail flickers against me. You use bones to make the broth.

NOAH BALDINO

Pep Talk

The vet tells me my new dog is exceptionally *food motivated*.
I, too, am very *food motivated*. I once throttled
down my throat an entire lifetime
supply of Nabisco Animal Crackers
just to get the lunch monitor to finally call me *The Ark*.
For only fifty dollars I would dare to take on the World's
Largest Marshmallow. Someone's called me that too.
But when I'm alone, I don't call myself anything. I like
to wriggle my way out of my mouth, to stay so quiet that
when I whisper *who's hungry* the dog wonders if she
dreamt the bowl herself. I suspect that last night
she tried to slip off my socks with her teeth. Here lies
a lone thread, laced around her snaggletooth, lilting
alarmingly in the morning breeze. Our attempts
for comfort keep me limber as a cheesecake, in the mind.
I doubt I'd eat a sock. At least, not a wool one. But who am I to judge?
All of 2010 I tried to take in meatball after meatball until
my dad wasn't dead anymore. It nearly worked—deep inside
I felt a gurgle and knew if I stopped precisely then I'd have
as many meatballs as he'd had years. I'm not sure I'm ready
to say his age out loud. But yes, that's how the dead speak:
a gurgle here, a grumble. If the dog pressed her ear to
my gut, I swear she'd hear a *hallelujah*. But she never listens.
So it's fitting, to talk with him like this. A trail of treats
to teach her to climb the stairs. A mint on the pillow of grief.
That whole year, I spent lunch on a bench in the dog park.
All sorts of breeds would sit beside me, my little disciples of meat.
Someone with a Pomeranian passed just as my fork missed its landing—
we made eye contact, thick marinara the wrong half of a masquerade

mask. I hope Heaven is full of people who look away in kindness
when a dogless stranger's lathered in spaghetti sauce. *Do you
kiss your father with that mouth?* they said. I thought them my Saint Peter.
I was silent then. But I have a dog now.

ALI SHAPIRO

Dogs in Love

I.
The dog who reminds us of you is easily wounded: every loud noise lands like a blow. She never barks but occasionally moans. The dog who reminds us of me has only two modes: all-out and asleep. She eats dinner out of a maze, has to be saved, every night, from her own appetite. She loves, in this order: food, tennis balls, you. Both dogs love squirrels, but once we saw the dog who reminds us of you leave an almost-dead one at the feet of the dog who reminds us of me, then slink carefully away. The dog who reminds us of me ate it.

II.
We break up, but our dogs don't. We pass them back and forth through various impromptu airlocks. I let them into your yard and they disappear through the back door, admitted by your invisible hand. You transfer them from your car to mine, then drive away before I get behind the wheel. Because the dogs have always been each of ours (your dog; my dog), and because they are each a part of us (daemons; animal familiars), the pass-through becomes a space where we are somehow still together, a world of what-ifs embodied and lovingly, grudgingly maintained.

III.
Our reunion comes with animal inevitability: a few drinks, flush of skin, clash of teeth. Then we're back where we started: cooking, vacuuming. Walking the dogs. The one who reminds us of me now insists on sleeping not just next to but *on top of* the dog who reminds us of you, who accepts the warm weight with a heavy sigh. Maybe it's true: opposites attract. Or maybe love is just knowing, no singular alignment of selves or stars but a groove one animal wears into another, slowly, surely, until the warmth becomes particular, the weight light.

IRÈNE P MATHIEU

there is no word for (my mother's fear of everything that might touch me)

I want to be your mother, little dog,
or at least give you unbreakable bones.

I shield your eyes from road kill,
pry discarded gum from your jaw
when you tongue trash off the sidewalk.
the day you first tried to howl I finished the sound for you,
and now there are times I howl quietly to myself
in the closet, hoping the neighbors will assume it's you.

the truth is that I miss walking on all fours,
your sense of smell.
I look you in the eyes and see behind language.
I press the tiny pulse in your paw to my wrist,
the spot we are most related.

when my mother curved her hand around mine
to make letters, whenever I smelled her
smoldering panic, I wanted to bury the word
bone in her paw. we wrote *shelter*. we wrote
shell. as if trying to bark ever bucked a bite.

       but it could—
think about it: if you said the perfect thing
you would never have to say anything else.
all howls therefore lead to more howls.
sometimes we find it easier to love a dog than

to love other humans, and we worry this makes us
bad humans. actually, we are bad listeners.

what kind of word is *bad*, anyway?
I buried it in the backyard, little dog.
I left the space where it was
empty, for once.

I should have stayed in that silent moment,
but I pulled you into my lap and uttered fiercely.
I was just teaching you to keep existing.
I wonder if I am a bad mother.
are you listening?
I just want you to exist.

EMILY ROSE COLE

Lovebites

The dog wiggles onto my chest, gums humming
the music of *bite*. She's just a puppy, so it's cute
when she clutches her jaws to the crest of my nose.

At least, Mama thinks so. *Lovebites*, she says,
as if the spaniel's need to chew would dull the reek
of her breath or ease the stitches of red I'll dash
with concealer before school tomorrow morning.
As if *bite* were inextricable from *love*. We both

grew up like that, Mama and I, thinking love
isn't love unless it draws blood—just like a dog
bite, so warm, so full of bright, bright teeth.

JASON MYERS

Spies
    Numbers 13

This morning I watched a hummingbird
steal secrets from the pansies I bought
at Home Depot, ransom them to the roses.
My privacy settings are out of date. *Unless
a grain of wheat falls into the earth…*
Our dog is dying. The day we adopted him,
when we swore we were going
just to look, we walked
around the base of Stone Mountain,
where laser lights flatter Jefferson
Davis, King's dream dead. *The Lord
said to Moses, 'Send men to spy out
the land of Canaan.'* We are told
it was *the season of the first ripe grapes.*
How long does it take land to decide
who belongs? How long before you know
a promise is kept or broken? *Promise
you won't die*, we would say to Gilbert
before we knew he was sick. Secrets
circle his eyes like birds wondering
is that my nest, is that my nest? The spies
took a single cluster of grapes, some
pomegranates and figs. I hate the hard
work of pomegranates, the agony
of each small hour of juice, time
in its political cells. *I may not get
there with you*, King said in Memphis,
there being Canaan, or wherever nectar

like water, like water flowed. How
many of his wires had been tapped,
Hoover convinced he was a communist
spy. How else to explain such vehement
displays of love, such oracles of
justice? When I say *nectar*, I mean
clean water, affordable housing, nobody
calling the police. Much rabbinical wisdom
suggests the language of Torah
is entirely code, an encryption
of divine lusciousness in each
woozy vowel, patient consonant.
Now, I write, *I can hold his dear
face in my hands*. Someday, though,
these will just be words. Every tongue
is a temple of ghosts. When cells
cross wires we call it cancer. When
night slips into night we call it
holy matrimony. The sounds of
heaven and the sounds of ache echo.
In Exodus, YHWH responds only
when the people cry out. Like we need
to know lack to know love. Like a body
out of tune learns a lighter melody. To
wander from piedmont to piedmont
is to revere, right or wrong, the summit.
Today's ripeness is tomorrow's rot.
Yesterday my empty hands held such promise,
       such promise.

LIZ BOWEN

Poor Stress Tolerance I

What they call irritability, I call a volcano.
I call out to the stranger who cut me off:
You're probably a fucking cop. I call out
to the stranger cackling in the movie theater
while a man publicly masturbates
to Emma Stone: *It's funny how women
aren't human.* I call out to the stranger
walking her breeder-bought puppy off-leash
in our building: *My dog will eat your dog.*
My dog will eat her dog if it runs up to her
because what they call aggression she calls
post-traumatic. Except she doesn't call it
anything, because she is a dog.
She has been bred to sagging udders
and dumped in a vacant lot. She has scars
balding her face and front legs. When families
see us coming, they cross the street. When
Upper West Siders put their accessory
animals in her path, it is she who is in danger
of being marked dangerous. My therapist
asks me why I identify with this creature,
what is the nature of our shared nature,
she and I who react.
                        A: The body holds
every failure of contact / marked safe.

LIZ BOWEN

Poor Stress Tolerance II

For three months after a man threatens
to kill my dog, my fingernails are brown
underneath and swollen, like ants have
made a home there. I pulled my dog's
mouth off his dog's collar with my hands,
without gloves. This is what humans
are not supposed to do during a dog
fight, because we could get hurt. I did get
hurt, because what else could I do? Keep
my culpable hands out of it? While the
blood streamed down my family's face?
I put my hands in the dog's mouth and
the dog's mouth pressed down against
my fingernails. For three months the blood
underneath pools and crusts and becomes
dry leaves, and I wonder when, if, they will
ever fall off. For three months I look at
my hands and see police lights, and hear
a man screaming that he will kill my dog
with a hammer if he ever sees her again.
For three months, I tell myself my dog
did not hurt his dog, and it is true,
but for three months I hear his voice
and feel the marbled implacable muscles
of dogs thrashing against my own torso
and I bludgeon that same torso with causality.
I was not careful. I made danger.
When the man sees my dog, he will kill her
with a hammer. I am in the car after three
months, driving back to New York after working

and recovering from withdrawal in Arizona,
like a tubercular eating dry air. Before I left
the city, I was afraid to leave the house
because the man would see my dog and kill her.
On the drive home, a new sensation surfaces,
unprompted: forget the rantings of a man
who is only angry he was made to feel
a single moment of fear. As I unpack my bags
the next day, the first fingernail peels away.

EMILIA PHILLIPS

My Dog Refused to Go Near the Dead Rabbit in the Backyard

after he got its smell. Brown like a toasted almond, with no
snapped neck or saliva

slick in its fur. Totally perfect. Except for the fact it was dead.

And so I suspected a heart
attack or a clot that had exploded into its brain like a bubble

in a lava lamp. The dog tucked his tail and watched from behind

my legs as I toed an ear
and then the whiskers, marveling at how they bent and how I could feel

only the slightest

resistance. I've had other dogs who would have killed
anything that moved across the yard

if they could catch it, and another who would have rolled

all over any rotstink, a smell that would revel in her wake even after
several hose baths, a sheen of almond oil.

Like all humans who have ever been shamed

by a belief or boys,
I have a hard time forgiving instinct.

By which I mean to say, the body.

Mine especially,
which I see in everything. The dead rabbit.

The dog, cowed and anxious.

Once, at thirteen, I laid facedown on the floor
where another girl straddled me to draw a dragon across my shoulders

with a green Magic Marker I tried not to imagine was anything other

than what it was
scaling up my back, wet and cold.

LINDA DOVE

The Dog Poem
for Gus

In this moment, dogs are not just dogs
but ideas. Epochs. Bridges between
the before-and-after shores. When
dogs go, the bridge collapses
into water that is something
like forgetting. Your ability to cross
back to the far bank is no longer
a matter of touching fur or hearing
some bark. Brown eyes pleading
for bone. This pleading, the desire
that you recognize as a part of the whole,
as having been there in all the houses
that run through you, all the dark
you have laid down in. But now you see
the before-shore as a distant, dreamy
place, as if you never lived there.
As if that life belongs to someone else,
who has a small, black-and-white dog
that follows her around, a desert dog
of granite boulders and canyons,
of cottonwoods in spring—the drifting
balls of fur—of chain-fruit cholla,
the fruit on fruit on fruit, like abacus beads,
like marrow, the way it keeps on going,
its one miscalculation of the world.

KUNJANA PARASHAR

Ritual

Mrs. Pereira had a dog named Rexi, who'd come after Ringo.
Rexi was frost-white in colour and used to follow me home, up to
the third floor of our apartment building. My mother would put out
a bowl of milk and bread for him. I never touched him because
nobody in our family did—we were not openly affectionate like that.
But his coming home was a ritual we took seriously, like appeasing
a god or goddess, like it'd be a shame if we'd sent him back hungry.
We couldn't do that when we'd been chosen by his reticent spirit,
his well-kept coat of fur, his old-man silence, his holiness—
illuminating our own.

STEVEN CORDOVA

Sissy Boy

When they first came, panting, begging
at back doors, grandparents laid out
scraps of food. Grandchildren stroked
a thin flank, a small trembling spine.
And they remained, nameless,
but fattened and multiplied.

They took to running in packs that barked
and turned the whole block in its sleep.

One boy dreams hunger, poison
hissing. He rolls off the bed.
A breath escapes in a rush across linoleum.

His own mother made the call.
Whining, baying, they struggled,
but they were nothing more than strays,
a haze of bristle and fur,
to be netted, caged.

Now the streets lay quiet, no howling
or mating. Trampled gardens unfurl.
Trash cans brim their empties.
And *mamasitas*—they sigh,
content without the sound of a wanton dog
defending itself in the middle of night,
fending off the fickle pack that turns on it,
the whimpering of the weak-haunched.

LIZA FLUM

Domestication

on a photograph of a Roman grave

Long jaw tipped
   toward a woman's chipped
anklebone, a dog curls

   her 26 ribs around a bowl
of pink glass. This grave
   is love's evidence:

that what lies at the foot still
   might rise and want a drink,
that the owner might rise too

   and find herself walking,
dog heeled, to the land
   of the dead: the dog

was deathless / they killed her
   the day her mistress died.
So we hypothesize.

   What we know of love
between species we learn
   from the bones:

some in middens,
   in trash heaps, bear the clear
marks of human digestion.

    My own mother loves
and takes in like this:
      she makes a dog's soft, dark

coat her burying ground
    for human loneliness.
I've learned her tactics.

    I hold my small dog
in my lap when I read *People*
      magazine: "I wanted my life

to be about not just me,"
    an actress says, holding
a baby in her arms,

    her red smile expanding.
I want expansiveness. In my arms
    my dog's little body

breathes and twitches
    in, I think, a running dream,
where he is alone.

GRADY CHAMBERS

Black Pomeranian

Whatever the boy's selling I don't want it, ducking,
as I am, into the car's cold cockpit, thinking already
of errands, post office, grocery, the bank's blank atrium,
keying the ignition when the photocopied face
of a panting Pomeranian fills the window.
Have you seen my dog? the boy shouts, and I remember
Buster, brutal, sleek, his black Labrador eyes, ferocious
and loyal in his delivery of teeth
into the face of a threatening neighbor.
I shake my head and the boy slumps off.

These days I keep those that love me at a distance
when once I clung to that dog's neck as he was strapped
down and punctured with a violence into sleep.
And I sigh, knowing later, driving the icy park road home,
I'll catch a glimpse of something black
limping into the thicket; knowing I'll then pull over,
knowing I'll walk the snow mounds to the edge
of the woods, knowing I'll bend down, kneel
even, knowing I'll peer into the dark scrambled branches,
muddying my knees in search of something gone.

LISA FAY COUTLEY

Leash Training

means trying to make my dog wear blinders
by shoveling fried hot dog bits in his mouth

that—jaws open & yawn wide—is the size
of a dinner plate sailing toward a woman's face

as she rounds her car to enter the bank
or a small boy pedaling his bike to the beach

baby toddling with kite ANOTHER DOG
swinging children who'll probably strangle us

with pigtails or tall grasses or they harbor
every barking friend he can hear all night

all drops of chocolate in the baking cake
he'll never eat if it doesn't fall to the floor

& who can blame him his lunge & buck
at a leashed end for wanting to blaze

an aspen grove after a herd of elk when
I can't make myself ignore a single detail—

the way you said my name or toward the end
breathed *yeah yeah yeah* until you simply didn't

LISA FAY COUTLEY

What Have You

Down here—forever projecting—
signs for signs for a sign for a woman

who kisses against the knife, but no one
sees her anymore. My son is the fist inside

the fist he's shaking at the rest of the world.
When he first heard his pocked heart homing

by rote, even its hollow couldn't show him
cage can also mean safe. Between us, clouds

are being torn apart by hands we can't see
or hold. Distance isn't the violent word we

mean if objects are always already absent.
What have you? What have you done

makes more sense. *What have you done for me
lately* doesn't make him laugh. What have I

done, he wants to know. Him. One of two
choices I made to hold change in the world.

II.

What have you *now*? I accuse the puppy
 & his boy responds—because desire
  Mom, because hunger—as if

he, too, could chew a couch cushion.
 I live here, with a head not made
  for hats, in blizzard country

where I accidentally slam the shovel
 against the asphalt & the dog
  barks & starts searching

for the other him & the other me. As if
 another us could be somewhere else
  where we sound better,

happier, full. My son says because desire,
 hunger, fifteen years already on Earth—
  this great gift he's certain we have

wasted & can never repair—words mean
 worse than nothing if we're thoughts
  unable to share pain

& wonder. What have you now to say,
 Mother, I ask myself, as I shove
  snow from an end to an edge

of dirt, bracing myself to throw, a language
 so old—what *have* you?—taunting
  me, the puppy arching, choking

on a chunk of anything, & I reach for a treat
 from my pocket to dislodge it, thinking good
  boy sounds so much like goodbye.

LISA FAY COUTLEY

Forgiveness

you want me to believe, means grabbing
some bolt cutters & setting myself free
from the chain that links me to
the dog that should protect me
but dragged me through the street
because every red truck is triggering,
so I started calling him father, mother,
waiting for the gashes on my knuckles
to heal, but hands, hands are so busy.
Even now, I can't forget how it felt
to pull my dead bird's feathers from
the bottom of a skateboard box on
a floor she couldn't leave like weeping
one's self to sleep forever. What does
it mean if a winged thing wishes for
a cage, if I boxed my bird & sank her
in a lake. Are you trying to tell me
I've buried my own song, that I've been
fooled by some second sky as seen
in a street puddle? I refuse to believe
my dead are still here, hearing me,
seeing me, yet when some baby bird
won't stop squawking & watching me
through my window as I'm about to bend
my fingers to these keys to say again
how angry I am that you did not protect
me but instead dragged me through such
ugly streets, Mother, I'm forced to look
away from my knuckles, to forget

my hands have yet to learn the kindest
way to handle me, because I know so well
this fear, this deep, young hunger, & I slip
Dad's old work gloves over my wounds
& rush outside to tend to a fledgling's wide
open beak with both hands & so much love.

RUTH BAUMANN

I'm Thirty Now, Poem.

There's a seriousness I've come to shun.
The moon could hang heavy or it could hang

or it could just be paused on its way
somewhere. I moved to Florida & ran

out of running. A body in rest asks
to be a body again someday, though.

The years for all of us exhale. Then
inhale, again. Last night in the parking lot

outside of Publix and a medium-priced
sushi place, I asked the man to make a wish

on the moon. Caught off-guard, he smiled
sideways & thought of his puppy, who walks

me twice a week through swamp bogs &
lakeside trails. Sorry to talk about the moon

so much. It's just an easy way to show you
how tides will do their work, brightly.

I've slept & I've slept & I've made beds
in the front & the back of my eyes, I've had

my rest. Sweet inland Florida, sweet
panhandle Florida, sweet October breaking

the neck of another late summer in Florida:
I'm awake. I even run with the puppy,

sometimes, lift my feet over branch
after branch after root.

RUTH BAUMANN

Reassurances

Weaning off meds, I have this electroshock heart all day &

it's okay, temporary. Today's reflection said *if you're disappointed*

in your progress, you're playing god, basically. *The only thing wrong*

with you is that you think something's wrong with you, I tell a friend.

Beauty tarnished is just beauty changed. Beauty changed is just

beauty made new. For all its fires, I believe the world is like us

& wants to grow slowly. I pray a lot for sturdiness, for faith

that props me up far beyond people. The puppy is sick but still

so cute he might be a cartoon animal, sniffing around in the incipient

spring, big-eyed & happy-tailed amongst fallen magnolia petals.

Nothing is immediate except turning my attention into care.

NINA SUDHAKAR

Commands in Progress

Look: it's night & I take comfort in your presence. Alone, I have never been able to control my level of visibility. Together, we are *brown woman with sizable dog* & I've found this visual encourages hesitation. A narrow slice of space just large enough for us to walk through.

Wait: I've learned, over time, to keep my promises. You watch to see what I still owe myself. The desire to be close bleeds into every breath—I see how the brain rewires to take notice. How tied up outside the store you wailed & wailed until you caught sight of my face again in the window.

Come: this field is empty & I delight in your exuberance. The joy I know is tethered to loss or anger or sorrow. I cannot yet manage your precise focus on the moment, this patch of soft grass, the open sky, the stains on your paws from diving full-tilt, refusing to relinquish perfection once found.

With me: your life, as any loved one's, is spanned by another. Aging condensed like a time capsule, shiny decade of our lives marked by your shadow. Any child we might have will wonder what you were like when freshly young & our minds will stretch eagerly backward: seeking to replay, settling instead to remember.

NINA SUDHAKAR

At Night

Tucked in nights beneath the mosquito nets
in Bangalore, strays holding forth their arguments

& roaming unfettered, pausing only for an eruption
of barks. With dawn comes freshly-nicked ears &

our morning walk, past dogs beached in sunlight
like rudderless whales, washed ashore & abandoned

because they did not know how to live out of sight,
how to die quietly alone. Raised like this

I could see that bringing an animal willingly
into one's house might cause alarm (each time

she yawns, I remember again her teeth). I grew up
instead among picket fences & houses hidden

from neighbors, amidst silence sold as comfort,
greens large enough for envy. A landscape

you could look upon & feel nothing but the living
weight of loneliness. So the closest I ever came:

a leashed stuffed spaniel that squeaked when pulled,
admirable in its obedience, a neatly packaged

concession. Years later I called & said
I'd finally done it, brought home an unknown

creature. I didn't say I watched her sleep
that whole first night, dream-squeaks

& twitch-kicks, bewildered by her mere
proximity. Where do they go when it's night,

I once asked in Bangalore, all those packs
that skirted our legs in my grandparents' sprawling

neighborhood. No matter, I was told;
we could always still hear them.

CRISTINA ANNINO

Il cane del buon consiglio

È un gigante il mio cane.
Mi porta il piatto sul collo,
il pane in bocca, è un maggiordomo,
mi dice di mangiare guardandomi
con fare d'uccello. Cammina
in bilico sul davanzale, ha pelo
di foca e quando salta pare
un giocoliere turchino.

Ora io dico:
qualcosa devo pur fare; nacqui
dalla bocca pietosa di un padre
e una madre che ammisero insieme
— hai davanti la vita preziosa,
restaci immortale —. Così ho tanti
libri. Cosa mi manca?
Lo chiedo a Diego che mi guarda
col bicchiere di vino in fronte.

Ce ne stiamo così sulla triste
tovaglia; io parlo ed aspiro
dalla narice la storia
del mio romanzo, ho lo stomaco
aperto, il cuore mi pulsa in fronte.
Diego squittisce col coltellino
sul naso:
non col sentimento, si capisce.

CRISTINA ANNINO as translated by ADRIA BERNARDI

The Advice-Giving Dog

My dog is a giant.
He brings me the plate on his neck,
carries the bread in his mouth, he's a butler,
he tells me to eat, watching me
with the penetrating stare of a bird. He walks
balanced on the window ledge, he's got
a seal's coat and when he jumps he looks like
a circus juggler.

Now I say:
I'd really better do something; I was born
from the compassionate mouth of a father
and a mother who together acknowledged
—you have a precious life ahead,
be immortal there. And so I have many
books. What do I lack?
I ask Diego this; he looks at me,
glass of wine in front of him.

This is how we remain, leaning on the sad
tablecloth; I talk and inhale
the story of my novel
through my nostrils, stomach
open, my heart pulsates on my forehead.
Diego squeaks with the knife
on his nose;
not with feelings, we get it.

KELLI RUSSELL AGODON

Hunger

If we never have enough love, we have more than most.
We have lost dogs in our neighborhood and wild coyotes,
and sometimes we can't tell them apart. Sometimes
we don't want to. Once I brought home a coyote and told
my lover we had a new pet. Until it ate our chickens.
Until it ate our chickens, our ducks, and our cat. Sometimes
we make mistakes and call them coincidences. We hold open
the door then wonder how the stranger ended up in our home.
There is a woman on our block who thinks she is feeding bunnies,
but they are large rats without tails. Remember the farmer's wife?
Remember the carving knife? We are all trying to change
what we fear into something beautiful. But even rats need to eat.
Even rats and coyotes and the bones on the trail could be the bones
on our plates. I ordered Cornish hen. I ordered duck. Sometimes
love hurts. Sometimes the lost dog doesn't want to be found.

MATTHEW GAVIN FRANK

After Grano Maturo
painting by Serafino de Tivoli

Desire is this coiled poodle,
its water bowl two days dry,
these mean burrs
holding to the sycamore. How
can we stifle this with baskets
on our heads, and scribbled
white dogs?

In this thaw, coffee cans
serve to measure dirt,
seed, snow, and tires
to protect a nest of bees.

You once said, this dog
is the same thing as time,
always running away after
the rabbits. Even so, we too
are planted in rows, grow
thoughtfully, into gunpowder.

These things worked once,
as you did, gripped with intention
and birth. Buried, your hands
somehow reach up still,
support what, from the street,
looks like a flag, You are still

strong enough to pull her jaws
open, slip the pink heartworm
pill inside. Soft enough to smooth
her throat into swallowing.

Still, you should know this:
when she passed in the community
garden, she did so beneath
a dead sunflower, bald, thick,
hunched, taller
than my real father ever was.

SAGE RAVENWOOD

Can't Branch

Dew grass. Sliver rays of sunlight refract
through shadow limbed webbing above the
dirt mapped path. I'm tugged onward in
a pup's favorite past time, the walk of all walks.
The morning has broken through night's limber
to daybreak walk. I'm awake and we're doing
this now, rush along walk. Along the wooded
path Bjarki, the golden bullheaded plow you
over beastly, stops dead in his tracks. In front
of the male domino, a single lone branch stick
straight up in the air. Let's give an eyebrow
raise for the tender sprout which dares to
give pause to a 65lb tenderfoot. *"C'mon, Bjarki
walk around the branch,"* earns me a sad-eyed,
amber pout proclaiming, he can't. He simply
can't with the branch on this glorious morn.
"You, can't be serious boug?" He's now bent
the branch ever so gently it's resting under his
chin. I sidle around my poor pup and branch alike.
To stand face to face with the most forlorn pup
ever to grace this place. *"Can't branch today?"*
I lower the branch tenderly so as not to snap
the fragile sapling, earning a pup's disgrace.
Tight lipped he bounds over, without so much
as a thank you ma'm glance back. Turning
around, I find Yazhi my Dobie coon, had once
again, let her mischief nose lead her astray
into an overgrown thorny hedge; where she

promptly got tangled and stuck as stuck goes.
Apparently, none of us can branch today.

CARRIE SHIPERS

The History of Dogs
After Dorianne Laux

Canus lupus familiaris, descended
from the gray wolf. Predators
& scavengers, pack hunters
with complex body language,
fused wristbones & tearing teeth.
Man's best friend. Bred to hunt
& herd, stand guard & carry burdens.
Crucified in ancient Rome,
slaughtered in Malta, flayed alive
in London to show how our blood
flows. Conditioned by Pavlov
to drool on cue, sent into space,
blinded for research & better cosmetics.
The only animal that can follow
finger-points, read human faces.
Curled on our laps, against our feet,
in the center of our beds. Offered
organic food, spas & cemeteries
all their own. Driven by hunger, will eat
human remains, even of those they love.

JENNIFER PERRINE

In This Dog-Eat-Dog World

I call Von *mon petit hamhock*, jiggle
her meaty thighs, *nom nom* nibble on her
upturned tummy, recall all those people
who, over the years, scrutinized my face,
deemed it safe to inquire, *Chinese people—
do you eat dogs?* When our pets misbehave,
my white partner jokes about which to roast
first come the apocalypse. While he sleeps,
Frank and Dash appeal to me, plead their case
until I agree my sweetheart would serve
as a fitter dinner, could keep us fed
for weeks. A girlfriend once quoted in bed
a dead philosopher, *love is when
you want to eat someone and choose not to.*
If I die at home, Comet will not yelp
for help, will consume me before I'm cold.
What weird pleasure to know my bones will feed
these shaggy beasts one last time. Long ago,
I asked an ex—at a party, no less—
in the event of my demise to rest
my remains in the forest, let wild wolves
scavenge what's left. My request wasn't meant
to be morbid—only to say, *why waste
sustenance?* Now, my pups whine at my feet,
feast on kitchen scraps dropped—by chance or not—

to the floor. When they first scent the new pooch
introduced next door, they snort and howl, bare
teeth, go tearing out toward the fence, ready
to dominate the Rottie who lumbers
over, twice their combined size, opens wide
to give each an aimless lick. If I could,
I'd offer this glimpse by way of response
to the gossip about the mom and pop
takeout joint in every town: I'd note how—
like our neighborly black and tan herder—
I go in, on occasion, for a taste,
press my lips to this bounty of canine
flesh. In return, I am blessed with their quick
nips. We don't need to bite, have already
sunk ourselves deep beneath each other's skin.

LEILA ORTIZ

Blessed

Maybe he dreams of playing in the snow. Or the satisfying feel of bark against gums. When his leg twitches and he whimpers, is he dreaming about a duck between his teeth, or a falling sun bruising everything in its path? He is love and nothing else. Almost the way I imagine god. While sleeping he can't guard me—he is belly up, vulnerable—also just like god. I was at Broadway Junction waiting for the L. The day was cold and bright. Standing on the elevated platform, I looked out at a cemetery across the street. My heart felt something old and hopeful. I was elated, blessed.

BECCA BARNISKIS

Saint Mutt

Back off a little when I have a fresh missalette in my mouth I tend to get erratic hey that was in good fun! Most times I adore you I move to put my paw in yours we bow our heads together to ask the Lord for one more thing. It's nice! This hymn is for sleeping. How about here? Or here yes better closer to the floor register see you in a little…did you hear that? There's a bird in my mouth I mean my mind did you hear that too? This carpet so good so soft. God is love and beef liver together the scent of moist garbage on the wind through the open window the sound of many cars being chased away. Don't trust the world or do—go ahead why not—to operate on its own accord. I guess food comes from somewhere water you have to search out daily. Pray hard don't pull practice for praise do good works everyday. Let's go. Let's go. Let's go. Let's go. Let's go. Follow me yes.

JEANNE WAGNER

Dogs That Look Like Wolves

When my dog hears the neighbor's baby cry, he begins
to howl, his head thrown back. He's all heartbreak and
hollow throat, tenderness rising in each ululation. He's
a saxophone of sadness, a shepherd calling for his stray.
I've read that baying is a both a sign of territory and
a reaching out for whatever lies beyond it: home and loss,
how can they be understood without each other?
Once I had an outdoor dog who sang every day at noon
when the Angelus belled from the corner church.
She was a plain dog, but I could prove, contrary to all
the theologians, that at least once a day she had a soul.
I've always loved dogs that look like wolves, loved
stories of wolves: the alphas, the bullies, the bachelors.
We have to forgive them when they break into our
fenced-off pastures, lured by the lull of a grazing herd,
or a complacent flock, heads bent down. Prey, it's called.
At night wolves chorus into the trackless air, the range
of their song riding far from their bodies till they think
the stars will hear it and be moved, almost to breaking,

while my poor dog stands alone on the deck, howling

into the canyon's breadth as if he's like me, looking

for a place where his song will carry. Dogs know,

if there is solace to be had, their voice will

find it. This air is made for lamentation.

JEFF OAKS

The Black Dog in the Middle of the Night

Sometimes the black dog wakes you up in the middle of the night.
Sometimes the dog is Anubis. Sometimes he's just your dog.
Sometimes you know something's wrong; there's
a terrible retching sound at the end of the bed. Sometimes
you just feel him looking at you, a physical thing
like a voice, and you say his name in the darkness.
Because in the old days there was a dark god who came
to guide you down to the place of judgement. There,
your heart would be weighed against an ostrich feather,
on the scales of the law in the kingdom of death.
Anubis the guardian of the dead and of orphans.
Anubis son of the sea and the underground.
Anubis the last face you'd see if your heart weighed
more than the law, before you were devoured
by Ammit, she who bursts, sometimes as a crocodile,
sometimes as a hippo, whatever you most fear,
out of hell's burning lake. The house is dark
and there is no noise from the street. You have still
not fixed that broken stair but you know how to
step over it by now. You remember where the leash was
and sure enough there it is again. A tail bangs into you.
It's your dog, and not Anubis. You are worried enough
about a number of things, you think, don't
make things worse. You have still not oiled
the hinges on the front door of course. It's
hard not to think it must sound to the neighbors
like a man coming out of a tomb, like some nut pretending
he is a god looking for lost souls. The dog
pulls you down to the abandoned lot where

all the dogs go to relieve themselves.
There's a temporary building there now.
Soon new foundations will be dug, upon which
new houses are planned for the well-off.
The black dog walks out into the new March grass
and pisses there. You look at the stars,
find the two planets in the news, forget which is which,
burning brightly as if in love. Not a single car
has driven by. You think, well, if this is my
last walk I think I've done good work in the world;
I think I haven't damaged anyone too badly, not
intentionally. I've tried to honor the laws of order
where I felt them in my heart. The black dogs
I've lived with, if they are called, if I'm asked for witnesses,
would not turn against me and shake me to pieces.
Then a perfectly normal car passes, and whatever death
it was you were preparing yourself for loses its hold.
The dog just wanted to pee, you say to yourself, get
a grip, stop being so willing to die, good god
aren't you a strange one? This time the hinges
on the front door sound old and you think
tomorrow maybe I'll finally go to the store and buy
some WD40 and make that creak disappear.
In the dark house, you find the treats on the counter
and give one to the dog who eats it fast. He's hungrier
than you expected; it may be why he woke you up.
He was hungry and knows the way to get fed this late
is to go outside first, follow the ritual of the dog
who deserves to be given something good in the night.
Very quickly after that he climbs back onto the bed
and his breathing changes. Leaving you to stare
out at the quiet neighborhood, wondering

where all this need to self-mythologize comes from
until the window stops being a mirror.

SALLY ROSEN KINDRED

Earth Science

I loved the Doppler Effect for Sam,
the Black Lab whose head shone
from the window of the red Ford

as Mr. Fenske drove past his pack
of students immersed in sun.
He drove by with his hand on the horn,

which was where Doppler came in, but better
was the black flap-eared bliss at the window
out of March, better the tongue's swagger

in the cracked-open air. We were thirteen,
viscous and secreting new warmth,
and this was why we were in love

with the earth, with its tender mass
of panting gratitude, its cool nails
ticking on the tiles under the padded weight

of an old dog's body, its hope as we'd stood up
before the tables black
with the study of grime

and watched the teacher open the dark door into spring.
It was early in the evolution of our flash
and damp in that small room. But now we were released

and Sam's tongue hung thick and pink, telling us
who we were: not Doppler, who thought he knew
how sound gave and withdrew; not sound

which wove between our bones in daring chords.
We were the dog, our hearts poured
from the vinyl heart of the dark car, our eyes sopped

in sun, tongues dipped in motion's sweat.
This was the reason we studied the earth, to learn
why air after rain smells like concrete and skin,

to talk about earth so it filled our wet mouths,
to let it heat our fine black fur
as we hurtled into April, space and time and sun.

AMY WATKINS

Clarity

A tire iron strikes the pavement and rings like a chime—
an accident, one pure note from the plain tool.

Nearby, one end of a red nylon leash in my hand,
I look up as though my love has said my name,

and for one moment the small universe that is my life—
me, my dog, his red leash, the row of beige apartments,

my family in their interlocking universes—arranges itself
around the unexpected clarity of that sound.

What follows is a moment of amplified silence, too brief
for a name in any language: the moment after waking,

a dream still real as memory, or the stillness after love.

JULIA STORY

The Last in a Series of Dog Elegies

Somewhere, your shadow walks
next to your shadow. Rare
maidens fall from trees, give you

the rarest kibble in a chalice
made of meat. I paint
your portrait under the couch:

your eyes dim as leftovers,
your pant as damp as lettuce.
Your dreams keep falling on you

as you lie twitching. In the night
something pounds in the trees
and you whittle it down

with your sleep. How will I prove
that I'd pick any scab for you?
A field runs out of the sky runs out

of the hose. Your teeth alone,
snapping. There is nothing
to scratch, to scratch with.

Your shadow next to your
shadow. There are only eyes closing,
spinning like cracked little bowls.

JULIA STORY

Barking

I planted lettuce while the farmer plowed something.
There was a loud whirring. I put each leaf
in the ground and dumped old rainwater over them.

I became filthy. The dog sniffed me thoroughly.
I let him. Then the whirring stopped and the farmer
went into the woods with a small wooden pipe.

Then the dog looked at me and became frightened, barking
as if I had offended him in the darkest of ways.
The bark was incriminating, ripe with anger, tearful.

He listed his troubles while I rocked squatting
on my feet. He barked until he was hoarse, until
I felt my eyes search the back of my head.

It was dark. I lay down in the lettuce. Where
was the farmer? I lay there until I began to bark,
and I barked until I knew something. I barked

into a lower place, where the dog's brown eyes
closed and together we entered a field of voices.

ASHLEY INGUANTA

Two Notes From a Far Off Watch Dog
for Piper

One: How to Run Again

It's 7:30am, and you are pouring a glass of milk in the kitchen. The tablecloth is red checkered, like on a TV show, and it's raining, and your brother is at the window with a telescope, looking at me, and he doesn't understand what he's seeing. That's okay--in three hundred years you won't understand either, and I'll be here, helping you learn how to run again. The field doesn't know that we call it so (yes, you remember), but it's in the way we say *field* now. Don't worry, if you can't feel it, I'm here. I'm teaching you to run in place, surrounded by glass, and you can feel me saying, *No matter where you are, you can always find me.*

When you took a look through your brother's telescope, did you understand the secret I dropped in your pocket? The one that would cause the whole world to fall into itself like a hail-rock dropping into a stretch of velvet ocean?

Tell me, when you say *glass* does a bird wrap itself around you, blocking rain?

When you learned what *gone* meant, did you allow yourself to cry?

Two: Patience, Faith

The space between your lover's hand and all wild berries became a constellation I penned you. We were in New York, and you saw it somewhere near the water, in West Manhattan, as the sun shone. I don't remember which day. It's not important. But sometimes I wonder if you understand the great load the field took. You ran to your lover with the weight of a great dane. You still do, but now the weight answers to *air*, and you feel it as you rest in bed, bra off, breathing onto a face that you'll only be able to find again through faith. I never knew what death was, but I believed in joy, so here I am--a star perhaps, something bright. The berries, they were periwinkle, and you looked at his hand knowing you'd one day no longer be able to touch it. Talk to me. I can show you how wrong you were. There's a napkin in the top right cabinet, in the corner. Fold it in half, press it to your bedroom window. Hold your hand to it flat, and wait.

SARAH LUX

Fleet Week

At night, surrounded in the starry
warm burrow of blankets and love and sex,
from the foot of the bed my dog gazed at her, steady, his eyes
dark pools of allegiance. He and I knew that she was
magic, he and I shared this devotion, we watched
her carefully like lightning, hungry-eyed and love, like you
inhale the scent of jasmine in the spring, like youth, like
storm chasing, like how you rest your palm
on the dying who are still so alive, how you chant the
invocation please
stay
stay
stay with me.

My dog, wrapped warm in coarse fur and hope. My dog, my heart,
he watched her, the good time, the one for whom he
somersaulted and cartwheeled, she like how an amusement park
ride turns you upside down, so that your soul drops to your head
and your brain drops to your foot.

Anyway, until the loud bang, the sharp thorn,
then my dog would hurry back to me,
paw offered palm up, needing comfort, seeking care.

My dog, he knows more than me about the world.

I leaned into her, nestled my nose in her armpit
that smelled of deep musk, emphatically her, just
squared. We fit. I'd followed her across the country.

I would have had her babies. We were in love.
She'd sent me a mixtape where Stephin Merritt sang,
Marry me. Marry me. My dog closed his eyes and sighed.
I whispered,
If I died, you would take him, right?

She laughed, a sound like music, and shook her head.
No, she said. No.

NOMI STONE

Waiting for Happiness

Dog knows when friend will come home
because each hour friend's smell pales,
air paring down the good smell
with its little diamond. It means I miss you
O I miss you, how hard it is to wait
for my happiness, and how good when
it arrives. Here we are in our bodies,
ripe as avocadoes, softer, brightening
with latencies like a hot, blue core
of electricity: our ankles knotted to our
calves by a thread, womb sparking
with watermelon seeds we swallowed
as children, the heart again badly hurt, trying
and failing. But it is almost five says
the dog. It is almost five.

Author Essays

C. SINCLAIRE BROWN

In the summer of 2016, I moved to Nashville to start grad school. The first things I did: rent an apartment and adopt this dog. Her name is Tilly. I found her online, on the website for a non-profit adoption group that rescues and homes animals throughout Middle Tennessee. I picked her because her picture was cute—Australian Kelpie (a farm dog), mostly black, with brown socks and eyebrows, soft brown chest plates and belly, fur slick and soft though with a bit of fluff around the neck—and because they estimated that she was about 2 and ½ years old, 35 pounds—perfect little compact thing, ready to squeeze right into my new apartment, ready to live at least as long as it would take for me to finish school. When I called to ask about her, they told me she might be difficult, that they didn't recommend her for a first-time dog owner. They said, when they found her wandering the streets of Jackson, she was all torn up, big wound on her leg, tail practically hanging off. They had to amputate the tail, so now she's got a little stub that only wags sometimes, when she really means it.

Tilly turned out to be a biter. "Mouthy," her foster had said. Meaning: she talks with her teeth because she was not socialized otherwise. She puts her mouth around my wrist and pulls when she wants attention, thinks a rapidly moving hand is an invitation for play. Sometimes she uses her mouth to say, *I am needy for touch and don't know how else to ask.* And sometimes she shows me her teeth to say, *I am terrified. I don't want to die. I am afraid you will hurt me. I will hurt you first so that I will not die.*

I know what it feels like to show my teeth in that way. When I write about dogs, I am writing about this. Her. How I see myself in her, sometimes feel those sharp dog-teeth in my own wild-woman mouth. When I adopted this dog, I had to put myself aside, listen to her, learn her language, her fears, how to talk to her in a way that she could understand. The whole process has taught me how to re-evaluate my own work, the work of writing into what is truly mysterious and terrifying and baffling, and letting myself simply be mystified, terrified, baffled. We do not speak the same language, Tilly and I, but we have come to some understandings. Poems are the same work to me. I mean: when I write, I feel like a dog, trying desperately to share a love, to draw a boundary, to come to some understandings with the world, with myself, especially in regard to past trauma and mental health. In this way, writing about dogs, and having this dog, have both been ways of feeling not-alone, of feeling sane.

CARLY JOY MILLER

One of my first dog memories is when I picked up Pepper, my family's Shih Tzu/Maltese, in the backyard while she was urinating and yelling out to my sisters, "Look, look! I finally get to hold her!" Of course, they were laughing, but I consider this moment one of pure desire: Little Carly was so eager to gain her dog's affection and wanted to seize the moment. Of course, as one realizes growing up, sometimes you have to wait for the love to come to you first versus trying to seize it so quickly.

While I do not own a dog currently, I've become the primary dog-sitter for many friends. I try to keep the dog on the same schedule while their owner is away, and since I work from home, it's pretty easy to do that. One of my roommates also owns a dog, and since many of our mutual friends own dogs, we host "puppy brunch" where everyone brings their dog and the humans get to eat together and chat about our doggy loves.

We have a saying that when a dog lays down on you, you're stuck. You can't move. Why ruin their slumber or joy? I approached the poem wanting to explore how far I would go to ensure a dog's comfort without going into too much sentimentality. I save the kisses for dogs in real life.

M. SOLEDAD CABALLERO

We were moving from a rural town to a city, and I thought it made sense to discuss giving Frieda away. That's a lie. I did not want to discuss it. I simply wanted to give her away. We had had Frieda for three years, and to my mind she had made those really hard years.

As a kid, I had always wanted a dog. When we finally moved into a house, my sisters and I begged my father to let us have a dog. Such an immigrant desire. We finally had a house, a dog just seemed like the obvious choice. Before this, the five of us had lived in rental properties, and usually dogs were not allowed. Such an American wish, a family dog, one that was ours because it meant we had space, we had enough money to care for a dog. We had "made" it.

Decades later when I thought I was an adult, and I was miserable enough at my first "real" job, I bullied my husband into getting a dog. *It will be so "good" for us I kept insisting. We can go on walks. We'll get exercise. I won't be able to work as much. You'll see.* When I think about that time now, I wonder how we both just showed up at the humane society, utterly unprepared (something completely of character for the academic in both of us), walked up and down the cages, saw this small skinny thing in a corner and took her home.

My panic about Frieda started on the ride home and almost never subsided. We got home, and I put the dog in the enclosed front porch, bit my nails, and watched her root around on wobbly, mud-matted legs. She felt monstrous to me, so monstrous that I called the humane society for weeks after begging them to take her back while my husband stared me down on the other side of the phone. These early reactions were not exactly about the dog, though at the time I would probably have punched you in the face for saying anything like that. She embodied my alienation about academia, about feeling alone as one of two LatinX faculty at work. But in those years, she felt like an alien creature who had imprisoned me.

I never got over or made peace with that feeling. I never anthropomorphized her; I never thought she loved us or hated us. She seemed her own utterly separate self. A mystery of fur, sad eyes, and enormous barks. I learned to live with and near her, and I did end up loving her. But, it was a hard, weird love.

When cancer grabbed her, I couldn't believe it. She's always been so big in my imagination, beyond deadly sludge cells, like a wild Medusa dog. When I got cancer six months after she died, I thanked her repeatedly. She gave me room to be sick without having to worry about her.

TARA BETTS

I grew up with dogs throughout my childhood, and they were often around to guard the house or warn us by barking at potential intruders. Sheba, a sleek Doberman Pinscher was one of those dogs.

When I was about 11 or 12, I had a dog named Mac who had white fur and he was part German Shepherd. He was one of the first living things that I had to be responsible for. I fed him, walked him, bathed him, gave him medicines for heartworm and such. I loved him and was heartbroken when my parents divorced and we could not take him with us.

A few years later, my mom bought a house with a big back yard in Kankakee, Illinois, where I grew up. I was in high school by then. She came home with a puppy that I promptly named Shorty, since he was part Terrier and part Dachshund. My mom got a second dog, a tiny female puppy, part Pekingese and part Poodle, that my brothers and I decided to call

Tiny. When they had puppies, we continued with the string of diminutive names—Micro, Mini, and June-June. I still miss those dogs.

Although I think some people value dogs more than human beings, I am still so grateful that I've had that experience to love and care for other living beings.

Aside from developing a deeper understanding for the interconnectivity of living creatures, I understand that as a child growing up steeped in Black history and Black communities, that people were taught to be afraid of dogs, which were weaponized against us during slavery and the Civil Rights Movement, but I also see how dogs are villainized with the same language that has been wielded against Black people. Like language and culture, dogs and other animals make our lives richer and maintain a delicate balance on the planet, but they also remind us how to be better, more thoughtful versions of ourselves.

RAENA SHIRALI

Like a dog, I follow our culture's commands concerning how to act in public spaces. I accept that I must avoid eye contact, look at the ground, look behind me, hold the pepper spray, hold the car keys facing out & spaced through the knuckles. I want to resist this conditioning but am powerless to do so. I have been trained how to exist in America, a country where we accept that masculinity is inherently violent, women are by default responsible for their own safety, and there is no compromise. I would be lying if I said I rescued my dog—Harley, a pit mix, who is around 75lbs and has definitely killed an opossum before—purely because he is the most handsome creature I've ever seen. Because he is also a signal, a deterrent, a kind of animal pepper spray. Here is my body in jean shorts and a crop top, yes, but here is the reason not to approach or attack me. This me is an us. This us has teeth.

Harley is there when I am alone. He barks when the mailperson slides envelopes through the double slots in the front door. He hurdles from kitchen to threshold when another human enters, his muscles rippling with effort, his hackles up. The dog is as concerned about my safety as I am, if not more. He is the only male entity I know who is this concerned about our territory, our right to exist privately and without trespass. He loves me unconditionally—& yet. Faye Webster sings, "I want to be happy…and get over how my dog is my best friend / and he doesn't even know what my name is." There is a power dynamic here. I train him like I have been trained to train him. He is my son and not an equal. I am skeptical of this social contract into which he entered without consent. Suddenly the culture of dog-parents spoiling our dog-children aligns. Anything to repay this unyielding protection. Any pig ears, any CBD treats, any leftover bacon. I am almost our culture. He obeys and I feed him scraps.

    & yet. Ours is a warm home. A Tempur-Pedic dog bed awaits him every night. In the morning he jumps up, nuzzles between my body & the body next to mine. Concerned as he is about my every move and which other bodies happen to be nearest to mine, he has no concept of boundaries—specifically, those between his body and mine. He jabs me accidentally with his huge paws. His ribcage outsizes my own. It curls around my spine and he grumbles into my back, annoyed that it took all night for me to invite him up into my bed. Some mornings this exchange makes me literally sob with gratitude.

    In his sleep he dreams of running without being leashed to my side. He kicks at me and I adjust his paws, curl my body around his. If we have to be here, if it has to be like this, I will at least promise him love. When we wake, we walk, and when I walk with him, the men don't say anything to us.

LIZ BOWEN

    These poems are from a manuscript organized around a cluster of psychological symptoms that I experienced while undergoing withdrawal from psychiatric medication. A profound and unexpected part of this process was entangled with my dog Rose, a rescue who has behavioral issues due to her abuse-marked past. Around the time I was most besieged by my own illness and resurfacing trauma, Rose's post-traumatic response to another dog resulted in an altercation in which she and I were both injured. While this incident was devastating to me, it was also deeply illuminating: though I'd always known that trauma lives in the body, it was another thing to care for this dog and witness the way her past took hold over her languageless body in unruly and impossible to disrupt waves. This witnessing both compounded my own struggle—as I was materially wrapped up in the things this dog's body made happen in the world—and opened up new paths for understanding and relating differently to my own body.

    Later, I began researching the scientific literature on the months-long physical and psychological ordeal that had ensued after I weaned myself off my meds. I was struck by one of the symptoms that typically characterizes what some researchers have called "persistent post-withdrawal disorders": *poor stress tolerance*. This was exactly how I had come to understand Rose's behavior, which, like mine, could seem unpredictable and threatening only if you didn't understand the necessary context—that is, the invisible mountain of stressors underlying each eruption of fear and desperation. The manuscript in which these poems are housed explores the set of new symptoms that arose for me only after I stopped my medication, and all of the poems titled *POOR STRESS TOLERANCE* deal with my relationship to Rose.

Though I can't exactly recommend that anyone else try training a reactive dog while going through withdrawal, I also don't know how I would have survived it without her.

LINDA DOVE

I have lived with dogs since the day I was born, and, of course, they mean for me all the usual stuff of deep connection and companionship to another being. Their devotion is legendary—their desire to please, their determination to prove their usefulness to the pack, their singular focus on you as their "person." And it is a two-way street, or it should be. One's caretaking of a dog is often a much less selfish project than the caretaking one does for one's human family. Dogs and humans give each other purpose.

But the longer I am alive—the older I get—the more dogs become something else to me as well and appear in my work, not just as actual bodies, but as symbolic embodiments. They are markers of time—and, for a poet, become time itself. They are representative of a past life, a life I left behind (except, of course, for my dog, who is a part of both). Forget coffee spoons; it is possible to count your life in dogs.

They are ghosts of places, too. In that sense, they are otherworldly. Here in California, much is made of the fact that dogs can apparently sense earthquakes before they happen, before the jerks and rolls clue the rest of us in; this eerie ability does not surprise me in the least, given the way they cross between the worlds of my mind already.

They have something to say about evolutionary time, too, the way that the historical intersects with the Darwinian; in a canine, that means evolving from wolves to dogs, and, in fact, is what gave birth to that poet's phrase, "the hour between dog and wolf," another way to talk about dusk, when the world turns dark and wild—as it often will in poems. Lately, I've begun to address that symbolic register in my poems directly. I might announce that *the dog is not (just) a dog*, as if I'm Magritte-ing the work.

Dogs can shape-shift like this.

KUNJANA PARASHAR

I often find a wave of love and some strange past-life loyalty washing over me when I see a dog—but I am shy and distant, so I do not give myself over—but I want to—I want to sit in the language of dogs and learn their private codes.

LISA FAY COUTLEY

The first time my Catahoula Leopard Hound pulled me across a snowy highway, I was fastening my snowshoes with one hand and holding his leash with the other, and I thought: *well, he's an eager puppy*. The first time he darted toward a dog he wanted to see through a chain-link fence, we were mid-run, and I sprained my ankle on a curb and cursed so loud the Mormon children waiting for their bus covered their faces in terror. The first time he lunged at a passerby, I was stunned and apologetic. The first time he dove for a moving vehicle, I feared for our lives. He was tethered to a 50-foot nylon line I'd coiled tight from my elbow to my thumb, so I'd have control while trying to train him to ignore distractions, when he caught sight of a hare in the long grass in the distance and tore after it, yanking me to the rocky ground like a ragdoll and dragging me at least ten feet. I was so fucking angry I made him stop and sit without a treat every two feet all along the long walk back to the car.

Only after Flanagan sprang at a strange man, who was standing at our door when I opened it as we were leaving for a walk, and said man kicked my dog in his chest and screamed at me, "Woman, you be careful, *woman*!"—only then did I call a trainer.

Russ had been a horse man all his life—trained them, owned them, rode them, loved them—and had parlayed that experience into a new career in dog training. Flanagan loved him because Russ was confident and he knew Flanagan was really smart but needed knowledge (and of course because he had a fanny pack full of fried hot dogs). Strangers assumed Flanagan (aka: Bubba or BubbaLove) was mean, but Russ could see he was a watcher, a thinker, and all of that data without direction terrified him—joggers, loud trucks, the erratic movements of small children, any man staring too long from inside an idling or parked car.

I had to give Flanagan more information to make him feel useful and more boundaries to make him feel safe. I had to teach him things I was never taught as a child—consistency, patience, confidence, self-soothing—and it took just one half-hour session with Russ to realize that training Flanagan was really about training myself. His flaws were my flaws—quick to respond to fear with force, loyal to a fault but untrusting.

    Loving and training him has taught me to be kinder to myself and to others. And as I have with the most meaningful poems I've written and read, I've gained a new perspective by observing and attempting to understand and to help him to reconcile and recognize safety from danger in an uncertain world.

NINA SUDHAKAR

    Having not grown up with a dog, but having always wanted one, it has been a revelation to finally have such a companion. My parents, who emigrated to the US from India, have a somewhat difficult relationship with dogs: my mother had one for a very brief period growing up, before she lost the dog to a road accident; my father never had a dog, but grew up with many strays around, which cultivated in him a healthy level of fear and suspicion. For me, raised in east coast suburbia, getting a dog seemed a missing piece in our assimilation to the so-called American dream. A proxy for demonstrating our harmlessness — *we're trustworthy! we love dogs, too!* — but also, a means of protecting us from harm. My desire for a dog built up over years, even after moving out of my parents', through different cities and stints abroad, underpinned by a constant refrain of "it's not the right time." It wasn't until a year and a half ago, the week my partner and I moved to Chicago in the dead of winter, that I recognized the fear beneath my avoidance: of what my family would think and say, of what I would have to confront about myself and my ability to care and be responsible for the needs of another, of the prospect of confronting inevitable, heartbreaking loss. That week, we adopted Siggi: a border collie/husky mix with boundless energy and an instantly calming presence. She reminds me not to talk myself out of the things I want, not to be cowed by burdens of expectation. To get out of my own head once in a while. There are basic needs to attend to: like the giving and receiving of love and care.

CARRIE SHIPERS

In the nine years since I rescued Sandbag, my eleven-pound miniature dachshund, I've written three books of poetry and a handful of essays with him laying on my lap or tucked under a blanket nearby. Because I prefer to write early in the morning, before I'm burdened or distracted by the day's mundane demands, it's not until after I've left my writing desk—and checked my email and polished my to-do list and (probably) showered—that I kneel beside the door with Sandbag's harness and leash and announce, "It's time to see the world," an offer he rarely refuses.

Over the years, I've gotten used to people in my neighborhood—first in Nebraska, then in Wisconsin, and now in Rhode Island—asking what kind of dog Sandbag is, then remarking on his distinctive brindle coat and especially on his short legs. The latter observation often leads to another question I've come to expect, which regards how far and for how long we typically walk. My stock answers, "Until we get tired," or "As far as he wants," are both perfectly true and designed to end the conversation so we can continue on our way.

Occasionally those same people comment that my dog is lucky to have such lengthy and regular walks. And while I appreciate the compliment, I also know that I benefit from them as much as he does. The world I see with Sandbag is different from the one I see when I'm by myself, even when I travel the same routes. This is true not only because of our pace, which ranges from sprightly to glacial and is prone, always, to sudden halts and detours, but because of the intense interest Sandbag takes in what he sees and hears and smells, whether he's investigating the strip of grass in front of our house or exploring a neighborhood we've never ventured into before.

As a poet, so much of what I do takes place inside my head that I sometimes forget the importance of being in my body, of giving my attention to the actual world rather than the one I labor to create on the page. After spending hours at my desk obsessing over where to place a comma or line break, it's a relief to simply be the person at the other end of Sandbag's leash, to serve the practical purposes of keeping him out of traffic and trying (and usually failing) to limit his garbage intake. And while I do sometimes return from our walks having solved a problem in my writing or having received the gift of a phrase or image that simply appeared in my brain without conscious effort, those occasions are always a bonus rather than a goal. For me, walking the dog—not merely seeing but truly experiencing the world—is perhaps the only activity in my life that feels less like a means to an end than simply an end in itself, and I am grateful for it.

JEANNE WAGNER

When, in retrospect, I look over my dog poems, I see that I have been writing about the boundaries and essence of the self. Dogs, evolved, so I've read, to be especially attuned not only to our habits and habitat, but to our subtlest facial expression. Dogs are found to gaze at the right side of the face, as we do, in order to better read our emotions. They've learned, to some extent, to discern and mirror our intentions and feelings. Another poet once told me I shouldn't anthropomorphize. But all poetry is transference, so why exclude dogs? They function in our lives as natural metaphors: of the wild, the infantile, the endearing. The other dogs I write about, like me, are lamenting the loss of their wild side, or expressing it, are frustrated with their boundaries, with us and each other, with a lost territory they can't reclaim. And their loss sometimes makes them sing.

AMY WATKINS

My family is fond of its dog stories: how my sister learned to walk by leaning on the collar of my uncle's rottweiler, how our German shepherd never warmed to the neighbor who turned out to be a predator, how my mom found her huge mixed-breed mastiff at the edge of the orange grove, starving and covered in ants, when he was a tiny abandoned puppy. I've known many good dogs in my life, but only one appears in my poems.

He was a small cream-colored pup when we brought him home from the Humane Society two months after our wedding. The shelter called him a "terrier mix," and all his littermates looked like Jack Russells. We expected a small dog appropriate to apartment life, but he grew quickly. At his prime he weighed 75 pounds and looked like no identifiable breed. Strangers liked to guess his ancestry; friends joked he was at least half Luck Dragon. Cheerful and scruffy and never very well-behaved, he was our friend and most devoted companion for 16 years.

He lingers in odd ways. Look closely at our daughter's first paintings, and you'll find wiry white hairs embedded in the acrylic. In the podcast I co-hosted near the end of his life, you can often hear his claws clacking on the wood floor, an irritating sound, impossible to edit out. And he's part of my poetry. Some poems reference him directly. Walking with my dog, I see something that triggers a memory or some reflection that incites the poem. More often, though, that happens off-page; he's been revised out of dozens of poems that would not exist without him.

I know there are extroverted poets, poets who engage the wider world in their artistic practice, but for me poetry is mostly an interior act. It requires external raw material, but I'm an introvert, prone to abstraction and living in my own head, not naturally inclined to go out and get the stimuli and experience I need to make art. On the small, day-to-day scale, my dog forced me to go outside and look at the world, even if it was just a walk around the block.

A dog is an ideal companion for a poet because they force us out into the world and because they stay with us when we have to withdraw from it. Sometimes my dog is a quiet presence at the edge of the poem, resting nearby while I write or read, wait up for a loved one, grieve. He died two years ago, and I miss him most when I wake up early to write, a lonelier act without his reassuring animal consciousness, undemanding but present with me in the dark places poetry sometimes takes me. I miss the weight of his head on my knee, calling me back to the light.

ASHLEY INGUANTA

Piper came into my life at a time when I felt significantly unloved. I was 24, just entering grad school for Creative Writing, and I wanted something I was not healthy enough to understand. At first, I sought this thing out in people--some sort of affection. And then I remember realizing I needed a different sort of healing. I began searching for dogs online.

I remember calling a pet rescue thousands of miles from my home, asking for a Maltese-Yorkie mix named "Makayla." I remember telling the woman on the phone I'd take Makayla everywhere, that she'd sleep on the bed with me, that I'd love her.

Why do dogs appear in my poems? Because when I picked up my dog from the airport, I remember holding most beautiful animal I'd ever seen, and how can I not honor her life as I honor so many other things--with the word, and the line, and music?

I remember not knowing what to call my dog--Makayla didn't fit. I remember running to the baggage carousel, a man peeking out from behind the curtain with a pet carrier, looking confused. I remember saying, "That's my dog," and I took her home with me. I remember going to bed that night, tucking her into her own bed beside mine. She found her way up to me without any help. Soon, I knew I'd call her Piper.

Why might poets particularly be drawn to dog companionship? Because when I found her, it felt like finding the words, but better. When I searched for her, it felt like holding my pen to the page, waiting, knowing something would be there. Poets know how to wait, and they know how to speak other languages. Dogs need that. They need people who can speak their language, because they can so greatly speak ours.

Piper died of cancer at nine years old. I remember walking with her in the Florida springtime--not too hot, not too cold--and the grass was so green. A woman walked up to us and said that my dog loved me.

Here are two notes from a watchdog, far off in the sky. Maybe this watchdog is light, or maybe she's a reflection of the boundless joy that radiates among us, that takes bravery to want, and to see.

Contributors

HANIF ABDURRAQIB is a poet and critic from Columbus, Ohio.

KELLI RUSSELL AGODON is a poet, writer, and editor from the Pacific Northwest. She's the author of six books, most recently, *Hourglass Museum* & *The Daily Poet: Day-By-Day Prompts for Your Writing Practice*. Kelli is the cofounder of Two Sylvias Press where she works as an editor and book cover designer. Her next collection of poems will be published by Copper Canyon Press in 2021.

NOAH BALDINO is a poet and editor. Their poems can be found in *Poetry*, *Indiana Review*, *Southeast Review*, and elsewhere. An associate editor for *West Branch* and the BOAAT Chapbook Contest, they currently live in Pennsylvania where they are a 2019-2020 Stadler Fellow.

BECCA BARNISKIS is a poet and performer. She has a chapbook, *Mimi and Xavier Star in a Museum That Fits Entirely in One's Pocket* (Anomalous Press). Other work has appeared in a wide range of journals including *Leveler*, *Scoundrel Time*, *Poetry London*, *LIT*, *Prairie Schooner*, *Conduit*, *Colorado Review*, *Vinyl*, *Typo*, and many others. She performs her poetry to live audiences regularly as part of the bands Downrange Telemetrics and Pancake7. More: beccabarniskis.com

RUTH BAUMANN is the author of *Parse* (Black Lawrence Press, 2018). She is the author of five chapbooks and a PhD candidate at Florida State University.

ROBIN BECKER is a Liberal Arts Research Professor Emerita of English and Women's Studies at Penn State University. She has published eight books of poems in the Pitt Poetry Series.

ADRIA BERNARDI is the author of a collection of essays, two novels, a collection of short stories, and an oral history. Her translations from the Italian include *The Rings of the Universe* the poetry of Ubaldo de Robertis.

TARA BETTS is the author of *Break the Habit* and *Arc & Hue* as well as the chapbooks *7 x 7: kwansabas* and *THE GREATEST!: An Homage to Muhammad Ali*. She is also part of the MFA faculty at Stonecoast-University of Southern Maine. Her work has appeared in numerous journals and anthologies.

LIZ BOWEN is a poet and critic living in New York. She is the author of the poetry collections *Sugarblood* (Metatron 2017) and *Compassion Fountain* (Trembling Pillow Press 2020). She is also a PhD candidate in English and Comparative Literature at Columbia University, where she is working on a dissertation that explores disability and animality as intertwined sites of literary experimentation in 20th and 21st century American literature. Liz is the senior poetry editor at *Peach Mag*, an editorial fellow at Public Books, and assistant editor of *Synapsis: A Health Humanities Journal*. Her recent writing can be found in *The New Inquiry, American Poetry Review, Lit Hub, Boston Review, TAGVVERK, and Cosmonauts Avenue*.

C. SINCLAIRE BROWN is a queer black poet and scholar, who was born in California, raised (mostly) in Texas, and is now living in Tennessee, where she is currently working on a PhD in English Literature and an MFA in Poetry at Vanderbilt University. She previously studied literature and poetry at Rice University where she was also the editor-in-chief of *R2: The Rice Review*. Her poems have appeared in *R2: The Rice Review* and *Poets.org*, and she is the current Visual Arts & Comics Editor and Poetry Co-Editor for *Nashville Review*. Catch her any day of the week eating too much food and spending way too much time chilling with (and writing about) her crazy-anxious dog.

M. SOLEDAD CABALLERO is Professor of English at Allegheny College Her scholarly work focuses on British Romanticism, travel writing, post-colonial literatures, WGSS, and interdisciplinarity. She is a 2017 CantoMundo fellow, has been nominated for a Pushcart Prize, a New Poet's Prize, has been a finalist for the *Missouri Review*'s Jeffry E. Smith poetry prize, the *Mississippi Review*'s annual editor's prize, and a finalist for the Lucille Medwick Memorial Award sponsored by the Poetry Society of America. In 2019, her manuscript was a finalist for the *Crab Orchard Review* first book prize, the Saturnalia Press first book prize, and a runner-up for the Autumn House Press first book prize. Her poems have appeared in the *Missouri Review*, the *Mississippi Review*, the *Iron Horse Literary Review, Memorius*, the *Crab Orchard Review, Anomaly*, and other venues.

GRADY CHAMBERS is the author of *North American Stadiums* (Milkweed, 2018) selected by Henri Cole as the winner of the inaugural Max Ritvo Poetry Prize. His poems and stories have appeared in or are forthcoming from *The Paris Review, Ploughshares, Kenyon Review Online, Prairie Schooner, Joyland,* and elsewhere. Grady is a former Wallace Stegner Fellow, and he lives in Philadelphia.

CHEN CHEN is the author of *When I Grow Up I Want to Be a List of Further Possibilities* (BOA Editions, 2017), which was longlisted for the National Book Award and won the Thom Gunn Award, among other honors. Bloodaxe Books has recently published the UK edition. Chen's work appears in many publications, including *Poetry, Poem-a-Day, The Best American Poetry* (2015 and 2019), and *The Best American Nonrequired Reading.* He has received a Pushcart Prize and fellowships from Kundiman and the National Endowment for the Arts. He teaches at Brandeis University as the Jacob Ziskind Poet-in-Residence and co-edits *Underblong.* He lives with his partner, Jeff Gilbert, and their pug dog, Mr. Rupert Giles.

EMILY ROSE COLE is the author of a chapbook, *Love & a Loaded Gun,* from Minerva Rising Press. She has received awards from *Jabberwock Review, Philadelphia Stories,* and the Academy of American Poets. Her poetry has appeared or is forthcoming in *Best New Poets 2018, Carve, and River Styx,* among others. She holds an MFA from Southern Illinois University Carbondale and is a PhD candidate in Poetry and Disability Studies at the University of Cincinnati.

STEVEN CORDOVA's full-length collection of poetry, *Long Distance,* was published by Bilingual Review Press in 2010. His poems have appeared in *Barrow Street, Bellevue Literary Review, Callaloo, The Journal, Los Angeles Review,* and *Northwest Review.* He reviews fiction and nonfiction for Lambda Literary. From San Antonio, TX, he lives in Brooklyn, New York.

LISA FAY COUTLEY is the author of *tether* (Black Lawrence Press, April 2020), *Errata* (Southern Illinois University Press, 2015), winner of the Crab Orchard Series in Poetry Open Competition Award, and *In the Carnival of Breathing* (Black Lawrence Press, 2011), winner of the Black River Chapbook Competition. Recent work appears in *AGNI, Brevity, Black Warrior Review,* and *The Missouri Review.* She is an NEA Fellow (2013) and Assistant Professor of Poetry in the Writer's Workshop at the University of Nebraska at Omaha.

LINDA DOVE holds a Ph.D. in Renaissance literature and teaches college writing. She is also an award-winning poet of four books: *In Defense of Objects* (Bear Star Press, 2009), *O Dear Deer*, (Squall Publishing, 2011), *This Too* (Tebot Bach, 2017), and *Fearn* (Cooper Dillon Books, 2019). Dove's poems have been nominated for a Pushcart Prize, the Robert H. Winner Award from the Poetry Society of America, *Best of the Net*, and *Best Microfiction*. In addition to her human family, she lives with her two very old Jack Russell terriers, Gus and Fiona, and several backyard chickens in the foothills east of Los Angeles, where she serves as the faculty editor of *MORIA Literary Magazine* at Woodbury University.

LIZA FLUM is a poet and teacher living in the Finger Lakes region of New York. She holds an MFA in poetry from Cornell, and her poems appear in journals including *Narrative*, *The Tampa Review*, *The Southeast Review*, *Lambda Literary*, and *The Collagist*. Her work has been supported by fellowships from the Saltonstall Foundation, the Vermont Studio Center, and the Kimmel Harding Nelson Center. She is currently a PhD student in Literature and Creative Writing at the University of Utah where she is a Vice Presidential Research Fellow. She works as a poetry editor for Omnidawn Publishing.

MATTHEW GAVIN FRANK is the author of the nonfiction books, *The Mad Feast: An Ecstatic Tour Through America's Food*, *Preparing the Ghost: An Essay Concerning the Giant Squid and Its First Photographer*, *Pot Farm*, and *Barolo*; the poetry books, *The Morrow Plots*, *Warranty in Zulu*, and *Sagittarius Agitprop*, and 2 chapbooks. His forthcoming nonfiction book, *A Brief Atmospheric Future*, is due out in 2021 from W.W. Norton: Liveright. He teaches at Northern Michigan University, where he is the Nonfiction/Hybrids Editor of *Passages North*. He persevered through this past winter via the occasional one-handed cartwheel in his mind.

CHLOE HONUM is the author of *Then Winter* and *The Tulip-Flame*, a finalist for the PEN Center USA Literary Award and winner of Foreword Reviews Poetry Book of the Year Award and a Texas Institute of Letters Award. Her work has appeared in *The Paris Review*, *Orion*, *Poetry*, and elsewhere. She has received a Ruth Lilly Fellowship, a MacDowell Colony Fellowship, and a Pushcart Prize, and she was a Grimshaw Sargeson Fellow in Auckland City. She was raised in Auckland, Aotearoa/New Zealand, and currently lives in Texas.

ASHLEY INGUANTA is an author, art photographer, and holistic educator who has been changed by the dogs in her life. Her work often focuses on romantic love, the spirit, landscape, and place.

SALLY ROSEN KINDRED is the author of *Book of Asters* and *No Eden*, from Mayapple Press, and three chapbooks, including *Says the Forest to the Girl* (Porkbelly Press, 2018). She has received two Individual Artist Awards from the Maryland State Arts Council. Her poems have appeared in *The Gettysburg Review*, *The Missouri Review's Poem-of-the-week web feature*, *Shenandoah*, and *Kenyon Review Online*.

SARAH LUX currently resides in the San Francisco Bay Area with her beloved fur kids. She works as a nonprofit fundraiser and worships poetry in her spare time.

IRÈNE P MATHIEU is a pediatrician, writer, and public health researcher. She is author of *Grand Marronage* (Switchback Books, 2019), which won Editor's Choice for the Gatewood Prize and runner-up for the Cave Canem/Northwestern Prize; *orogeny* (Trembling Pillow Press, 2017), which won the Bob Kaufman Book Prize; and *the galaxy of origins* (dancing girl press & studio, 2014). Irène has received fellowships from the Fulbright Foundation, Callaloo Creative Writing Workshop, and Virginia Center for the Creative Arts. A poetry book reviewer for *Muzzle Magazine* and an editor for the *Journal of General Internal Medicine*'s humanities section, she is represented by Jack Jones Literary Arts.

CARLY JOY MILLER is the author of *Ceremonial* (Orison Books, 2018), selected by Carl Phillips as the winner of the 2017 Orison Prize for Poetry, and the chapbook *Like a Beast* (Anhinga Press, 2017), winner of the 2016 Rick Campbell Prize. Her work has appeared in *The Adroit Journal*, *Blackbird*, *Boston Review*, *Gulf Coast*, *West Branch* and elsewhere. She is a co-director of the *Adroit Journal* Summer Mentorship Program.

JASON MYERS serves as Editor-in-Chief of *The EcoTheo Review*. A National Poetry Series Finalist, his poems have appeared widely including in *The Believer*, *The Paris Review*, *West Branch*, and *American Poet*, in which they were introduced by Campbell McGrath. He works as a hospice chaplain around Austin, Texas, where he lives with his wife and son.

JEFF OAKS' debut book of poetry, *Little What*, was published by Lily Poetry Review Books. He has published poems most recently in *Best New Poets, Field, Georgia Review, Missouri Review, Superstition Review*, and *Tupelo Quarterly*. His essays have appeared in *At Length, Creative Nonfiction, Fourth Genre, Kenyon Review Online*, and *Water~Stone Review*. Work has also appeared in the anthologies *Brief Encounters: A Collection of Contemporary Nonfiction*, and *My Diva: 65 Gay Men on the Women Who Inspire Them*. He teaches writing at the University of Pittsburgh.

LEILA ORTIZ is a poet and social worker in NYC public schools. Born and raised in New York City Leila currently resides in park slope. Her work has appeared in numerous publications including *Sixth Finch, Tinderbos*, and *Apogee*. Leila is the author of two chapbooks *Girl Life* (Recreation League, 2016) and *A Mouth is Not a Place* (Dancing Girl Press, 2017). She is a journal editor at *No, Dear Magazine*.

KUNJANA PARASHAR is a poet living in Mumbai. She holds an MA in English Literature from Mumbai University. Her poems appear or are forthcoming in *Borderlands, UCity Review, Lammergeier, Cha, The Hellebore, The Rumpus* (Enough section), *Camwood Literary Magazine, Glintmoon*, and elsewhere.

JENNIFER PERRINE is the author of three books of poetry: *No Confession, No Mass* (winner of the Publishing Triangle Audre Lorde Award and the Prairie Schooner Book Prize); *In the Human Zoo*; and *The Body Is No Machine*. A fourth book, *Again*, is forthcoming from Airlie Press in 2020. Jennifer's recent poetry and fiction appear in *Rattle, Salt Hill, Arc Poetry Magazine, Pleiades, Crazyhorse*, and *Valparaiso Fiction Review*, as well as in Broadsided Press' special folio, "Bearing Arms: Responding to Guns in American Culture." Jennifer is a recipient of the 2019 Oregon Poetry Community Fellowship from Literary Arts. They work as the Program Director for College Possible Oregon and teach writing through community workshops and the Writers in the Schools program in Portland.

EMILIA PHILLIPS is the author of three poetry collections from the University of Akron Press, most recently *Empty Clip* (2018), and four chapbooks, including *Hemlock* (Diode Editions, 2019). Her poems and lyric essays appear widely in literary publications including *Agni, American Poetry Review, Gulf Coast, The Kenyon Review, New England Review, Ploughshares*,

Poetry, and elsewhere. She's an Assistant Professor in the MFA Writing Program and the Department of English at the University of North Carolina at Greensboro.

SAGE RAVENWOOD is a deaf Cherokee woman residing in upstate NY with her two rescue dogs, Bjarki and Yazhi, and her one-eyed cat Max. She is an outspoken advocate against animal cruelty and domestic violence. Her work can be found in *Glass Poetry - Poets Resist.*

ROSALIE MOFFETT is the author of *Nervous System,* winner of the National Poetry Series, chosen by Monica Youn, forthcoming from Harper Collins/Ecco press. She is also the author of *June in Eden,* winner of the Ohio State University Press/The Journal prize. She has been awarded the "Discovery"/Boston Review prize, a Wallace Stegner Fellowship in Creative Writing from Stanford University, and scholarships from the Tin House and Bread Loaf writing workshops. Her poems and essays have appeared in *Tin House, The Believer, FIELD, Narrative, Kenyon Review, Agni, Ploughshares,* and other magazines, as well as in the anthology "Gathered: Contemporary Quaker Poets." She is an Assistant Professor at the University of Southern Indiana.

ALI SHAPIRO teaches writing at the University of Michigan's Stamps School of Art & Design. Her comics, poems, essays and reviews have appeared in *Gertrude, Muzzle, Prairie Schooner, The Rumpus,* and *Electric Literature,* among others. More work is available on her website, ali-shapiro.com, and pictures of her dogs are available on their Instagram, @twobrindles.

CARRIE SHIPERS's poems have appeared in *Crab Orchard Review, Hayden's Ferry Review, New England Review, North American Review, Prairie Schooner, The Southern Review,* and other journals. She is the author of *Ordinary Mourning* (ABZ, 2010), *Cause for Concern* (Able Muse, 2015), *Family Resemblances* (University of New Mexico, 2016), and *Grief Land* (University of New Mexico, forthcoming).

RAENA SHIRALI is the author of *GILT* (YesYes Books, 2017), which won the 2018 Milt Kessler Poetry Book Award. She is the recipient of a Pushcart Prize, a 2019 PEN America Writer's Emergency Fund Grant, a 2018 VIDA scholarship, a 2017 Philip Roth Residency at Bucknell University, and a "Discovery"/Boston Review Poetry Prize in 2013. Her poems have also received prizes from *Cosmonauts Avenue* in 2016 and *Gulf Coast* in 2014. Shirali's poems & reviews have appeared widely in *American Poetry Review, Academy of American Poets' Poem-A*

Day, The Nation, The Rumpus, & elsewhere. She recently co-organized We (Too) Are Philly—a summer poetry festival highlighting voices of color—and serves as Poetry Editor for *Muzzle Magazine.* Shirali lives in Philadelphia, where she is an Assistant Professor of English at Holy Family University.

MAGGIE SMITH is the author of four books, including *Good Bones* (Tupelo Press 2017) and *Keep Moving: Notes on Loss, Creativity, and Change* (One Signal/Simon & Schuster 2020). Smith's work has appeared or is forthcoming in the *New York Times, The New Yorker, Tin House, POETRY,* and the *Paris Review.*

BRUCE SNIDER is the author of three poetry collections—*Fruit; Paradise, Indiana;* and *The Year We Studied Women.* He is co-editor of *The Poem's Country: Place and Poetic Practice.* His poems and essays have appeared in the *American Poetry Review, Harvard Review, Iowa Review, Kenyon Review, New England Review, POETRY, Threepenny Review* and *Best American Poetry,* among others. He's currently an Associate Professor at the University of San Francisco.

NOMI STONE is a poet and an anthropologist, and the author of two poetry collections, *Stranger's Notebook* (TriQuarterly 2008) and *Kill Class* (Tupelo 2019). Winner of a Pushcart Prize, Stone's poems appear recently in *POETRY, American Poetry Review, The New Republic, The Best American Poetry, Tin House, New England Review,* and elsewhere. She has a PhD in Anthropology from Columbia and an MFA in Poetry from Warren Wilson, and she is an Assistant Professor in Poetry at the University of Texas, Dallas.

JULIA STORY is the author of *Post Moxie* (Sarabande Books), *Spinster for Hire* (forthcoming 2020), and the chapbooks *The Trapdoor* (dancing girl press) and *Julie the Astonishing* (Sixth Finch Books). She is a recipient of a Pushcart Prize and her recent work can be read in *Sixth Finch, Tinderbox,* and *Tupelo Quarterly.* She is a Midwesterner who now lives in Massachusetts.

NINA SUDHAKAR is a writer, poet, and lawyer based in Chicago. She is the author of the poetry chapbooks *Matriarchetypes* (winner of the 2017 Bird's Thumb Poetry Chapbook Contest) and *Embodiments* (forthcoming from Sutra Press). Her work has appeared in *The Offing, Ecotone, Tinderbox Poetry Journal,* and elsewhere.

JEANNE WAGNER is the winner of several national awards including the Arts & Letters Award, and Sow's Ear prize for an individual poem. Her poems have appeared in *Cincinnati Review*, *Alaska Quarterly Review*, *North American Review*, *Southern Review* and *Shenandoah*. She has four chapbooks and two full-length collections: *The Zen Piano-mover*, winner of the Stevens Prize, and *In the Body of Our Lives*, published by Sixteen Rivers Press. Her latest manuscript, *Everything Turns into Something Else*, will be published in the spring of 2020 as runner-up in the Grayson Book Prize.

AMY WATKINS is the author of the chapbooks *Milk & Water*, *Lucky*, and *Wolf Daughter*. She lives in Orlando with her husband and daughter and a mean-spirited ginger cat.

CANDACE WILLIAMS, by day, is a sixth-grade humanities educator and robotics coach. By night and subway ride, they are a poet. Their chapbook, *Spells for Black Wizards*, was a 2017 TAR Chapbook Series winner and published by the Atlas Review. The second edition of *Spells for Black Wizards* was released in 2019. *futureblack*, their first full-length poetry manuscript, was a 2018 National Poetry Series finalist.

Reprint Credits

Noa Baldino: "On Trust," and "Pep Talk," *Adroit Journal*. Reprinted by permission of the author.

Becca Baniskis: "Saint Mutt," *Colorado Review*. Reprinted by permission of the author.

Robin Becker: "Xenia," *Slate*. Reprinted by permission of the author.

Adria Bernardi: "Il cane del buon consiglio / The Advice-Giving Dog," *Chronic Hearing Selected*. Reprinted by permission of the author.

Steven Cordova: "Sissy Boy," *Borderlands: Texas Poetry Review*. Reprinted by permission of the author.

Lisa Fay Coutley: "Leash Training," *Blackbird*; "What Have You," *Dialogist*. Reprinted by permission of the author.

Liza Flum: "Domestication," *Narrative Magazine*. Reprinted by permission of the author.

Chloe Honum: "The Ward Above," *Copper Nickel*; "Phoebe," *Salamander*. Reprinted by permission of the author.

Kelli Russell Agodon: "Hunger," *Poets.org*. Reprinted by permission of the author.

Sally Rosen Kindred: "Earth Science," *MayApple Press*. Reprinted by permission of the author.

Rosalie Moffett: "New Evidence of Water," *Pleiades*; "Something Quiet," *Southern Indiana Review*; "How Is She? I Don't Say I Am Afraid," *Beloit Poetry Journal*. Reprinted by permission of the author.

Ali Shapiro: "Dogs in Love," *Electric Literature*. Reprinted by permission of the author.

Carrie Shipers: "The History of Dogs," *The Fiddleback*. Reprinted by permission of the author.

Raena Shirali: "PASTORAL WITH KEYS CLENCHED, AS A WEAPON, IN MY FIST," *bedfellows*. Reprinted by permission of the author.

Maggie Smith: "Walking the Dog," *AGNI*; "The Village Dogs," *American Poetry Review*. Reprinted by permission of the author.

Bruce Snider: "DEVOTIONS," *POETRY*. Reprinted by permission of the author.

Julia Story: "Barking," *Painted Bride Quarterly*. Reprinted by permission of the author.

Jeanne Wagner: "Dogs That Look Like Wolves," *Nimrod International Journal*. Reprinted by permission of the author.

Candace Williams: "Crown Heights," *Brooklyn Poets*. Reprinted by permission of the author.

THANK YOU

Ruth and Rachel would like to thank Erin Elizabeth Smith and the Sundress Publications team for believing in this project and helping us to bring it to life.

Thank you to each and every author featured in these pages for trusting us with your stories and poems, for sharing in the joy of creating this. That we personally can't set down this collection is a testament to your generosity and craft.

We'd also like to thank our dear friend Katie Oldaker for inspiring the idea for this anthology after a reading in Pittsburgh after meeting our dogs. Thank you for seeing this potential in us before we recognized it ourselves.

Ruth would like to thank Rachel for being a brilliant co-editor and friend. It was inspiring to work so closely with you and to see your great mind at work. She also thanks Eric Shonkwiler, great love of her life, for his support and encouragement while she read thousands of poems and cried a lot. And boundless gratitude to her dogs Bowie, Winnie, Asher, and Bub, and her ghost dogs Pete and Tobi. Your love has made her better at every turn.

Rachel would like to thank Ruth for agreeing to undertake this project together and seeing it through one email, idea, and poem at a time. Ruth, reading alongside you has taught this poet to be a more attentive, compassionate editor and—unquestionably—a better person. Thanks to Rachel's spouse Nick Goodmanson for each of Otto's thousand perfect nicknames, which she promises never to publish. Above all, gratitude to Otto: to those spindly legs and your long hound-snout; for your ongoing lessons in unconditional love and your constant guidance towards my survival.

Editors

RUTH AWAD is the Lebanese-American author of *Set to Music a Wildfire* (Southern Indiana Review Press, 2017), winner of the 2016 Michael Waters Poetry Prize and the 2018 Ohioana Book Award for Poetry. She is the recipient of a 2016 Ohio Arts Council Individual Excellence Award and won the 2013 and 2012 Dorothy Sargent Rosenberg Poetry Prize and the 2011 *Copper Nickel* Poetry Contest. Her work appears or is forthcoming in *Poetry, Poem-a-Day, The Believer, The New Republic, Pleiades, The Missouri Review, The Rumpus*, and elsewhere. She has an MFA in poetry from Southern Illinois University Carbondale, and she lives and writes in Columbus, Ohio, with her four bratty and joyous Pomeranians.

RACHEL MENNIES is the author of *The Naomi Letters*, forthcoming from BOA Editions in 2021, and *The Glad Hand of God Points Backwards*, the 2014 winner of the Walt McDonald First-Book Prize in Poetry and finalist for a National Jewish Book Award. Her poetry has appeared at *The Believer, Kenyon Review*, and *American Poetry Review*, and her nonfiction has appeared at *The Millions, The Poetry Foundation*, and *LitHub*, among other outlets. Mennies took over for Robert Fink in 2016 as the series editor of the Walt McDonald First-Book Prize in Poetry at Texas Tech University Press; she also serves as the reviews editor for *AGNI*. She lives in Chicago, where she works as a freelance editor and writer, with her spouse and her rescue greyhound mix, Otto.

OTHER SUNDRESS ANTHOLOGIES

Political Punch: Contemporary Poems on the Politics of Identity
Edited by Fox Frazier-Foley and Erin Elizabeth Smith
$20

Till the Tide: An Anthology of Mermaid Poetry
Edited by Trista Edwards
$18

Not Somewhere Else But Here: A Contemporary Anthology of Women and Place
Edited by Erin Elizabeth Smith, T.A. Noonan, Rhonda Lott, and Beth Couture
$20

Gathered: Contemporary Quaker Poets
Edited by Nick McRae
$16

www.ingramcontent.com/pod-product-compliance
Lightning Source LLC
Chambersburg PA
CBHW080452170426
43196CB00016B/2777